Contents

1 What Is Strength Training?   1

2 Scientific Strength Training:
   Muscles and Your Sport   15

3 Tips and Techniques for
   Effective Strength Training   27

4 Injuries:
   Prevention and Rehabilitation   67

5 Level One:
   Beginning Strength Training   75

6 Level Two:
   Intermediate Strength Training   155

7 Level Three:
   Advanced Strength Training   247

8 Individualized Sports Programs   305

   Aikido   307
   Alpine Skiing   308
   Archery   308
   Badminton   308
   Baseball   309
   Basketball   310

Bicycling	311
Bowling	312
Boxing	313
Canoeing	314
Climbing	315
Crew	316
Diving	317
Equestrian Events	317
Fencing	318
Field Hockey	319
Football	320
Golf	321
Gymnastics	321
Handball	322
Hiking	322
Hockey	323
Judo	324
Karate/Kung Fu	325
Kayaking	326
Nordic Skiing	
Cross-country	326
Jumping	327
Racquetball	328
Rugby	329
Running	330
Skating	
Figure or Ice	331
Roller	331
Speed	331
Skiing	332
Skin Diving	333
Soccer	334
Softball	334
Squash	335
Swimming	336
Tennis	337
Track and Field	
Decathlon/Pentathlon	338
Longer Runs	338
Short Runs	339
Throws	340

STRENGTH TRAINING IS EFFICIENT

With relatively brief work-outs, you will see and feel the remarkable difference in your performance.

STRENGTH TRAINING IS EFFECTIVE

You will develop the exact muscles you need for the sport you choose—and also gain in flexibility, avoiding the dangers of being "muscle-bound."

STRENGTH TRAINING IS SAFE

Not only does the Gold's Gym program allow you to build up your body without tearing yourself apart, but the strength you gain will also protect you against athletic injuries.

STRENGTH TRAINING IS FOR YOU

Join the new generation of sports-minded people using today's "miracle machines"—and become the winner you want to be.

COMPLETE FOR NAUTILUS, FREE WEIGHT AND UNIVERSAL GYMS!

Berkley Books by Ken Sprague

THE GOLD'S GYM BOOK OF STRENGTH TRAINING FOR ATHLETES
THE GOLD'S GYM WEIGHT TRAINING BOOK
(With Bill Dobbins)

THE

GOLD'S GYM

BOOK OF

STRENGTH TRAINING FOR ATHLETES

*Building a
Sports-Effective
Body For
Men and Women*

KEN SPRAGUE

BERKLEY BOOKS, NEW YORK

THE GOLD'S GYM BOOK OF STRENGTH
TRAINING FOR ATHLETES

A Berkley Book / published by arrangement with
J. P. Tarcher, Inc.

PRINTING HISTORY
Tarcher edition published 1979
Berkley edition / October 1981
Third printing / June 1983

ISBN: 0-425-05065-3

A BERKLEY BOOK ® TM 757,375
Berkley Books are published by Berkley Publishing Corporation,
200 Madison Avenue, New York, New York 10016.
The name "BERKLEY" and the stylized "B" with design
are trademarks belonging to Berkley Publishing Corporation.
PRINTED IN THE UNITED STATES OF AMERICA

We wish to thank Sean Harrington
and the staff of the
Nautilus Fitness and Training Center
for their help and consideration.

To Kenny and Julie

Volleyball   341
Water Polo   342
Water Skiing   343
Wrestling   344
Wrist Wrestling   344

9 Superstrength and Superendurance   347

10 The Strength Coach   357

Suggested Reading   362

Index   364

What Is Strength Training? 1

Anyone who is serious about wanting to improve athletic performance can do so at any age with strength training. Whether you're ten years of age or seventy and above, male or female, a weekend softball player or a seasoned professional superstar, once you have made the decision to improve, once you have made the inner commitment to excel, strength training will enable you to reach that goal. And you have undoubtedly made this commitment, because you are now reading this book.

At some time in every athlete's search for improvement comes the decision to train for strength, because strength is one of the many components that make up athletic ability. Strength in a sport can be developed exactly like flexibility or endurance; and once developed, it can combine with the other qualities you have sought to improve to help you maximize your inherent athletic potential.

Over the past ten years, Gold's Gym has helped the thousands of men and women who have trained there to become better athletes. Both professional and amateur athletes—as well as individuals from such diverse walks of life as medicine, business, education, and housewifery—have come to the most famous strength-building gym in the world to learn from the experts.

While Gold's has gained an international reputation as the gym where famous bodybuilders like Arnold "Pumping Iron"

Schwarzenegger and Lou "The Incredible Hulk" Ferrigno have trained, a far greater percentage of the gym's members are high school, college, and professional athletes, as well as average men, women, and children just seeking to become physically fit. But it isn't necessary to train at Gold's Gym to benefit from its proven expertise, because with this book you can turn any weight room into your own Gold's Gym. And this weight room can be your bedroom, garage, basement, school gym, health spa, or magnificently equipped commercial gymnasium.

Where you strength train is far less important than *how* you train, so in this book you will learn the proven Gold's Gym method of strength training. Every exercise, every training technique, and every workout has been tested on Gold's Gym members and proven to be effective in improving individual sports performance. If you follow the recommended procedures you, too, will increase your athletic skill by improving your strength.

STRENGTH TRAINING AND SPORTS PERFORMANCE

Strength training—training with some form of weighted resistance—gradually strengthens your skeletal muscles. These muscles move your body, both perceptibly and imperceptibly, in myriad directions, allowing you to put yourself into any body position or do any movement needed in your athletic activity. When your muscles are stronger, you assume such positions and make such movements more easily and efficiently.

Strength training takes many forms: exercising with weights attached to your ankles, wrists, or waist; running up stairs; swimming with your arms while pulling a float board with your legs; doing calisthenics; or doing isometric contractions against an immovable object. This book deals primarily with weight training. Furthermore, the training programs are geared almost exclusively to the use of free weights (barbells, dumbells, and related equipment), Universal Gyms, and Nautilus machines, because these are by far the most common modes of strength

training and are used by the majority of athletes.

Generally speaking, the terms *strength training, weight training*, and *heavy-resistance exercise* will be used interchangeably. When other modes of strength training—such as isometrics—are mentioned, they will be clearly explained.

Regardless of the method you use to apply resistance, you will build strength. Strength is one of the numerous components that contribute to your athletic ability. Among the other components are inherited physical factors such as height, bone lengths, and body leverages; speed; endurance; reaction time; psychological preparedness; flexibility; and movement pattern skills. Of all the components of your athletic ability, strength can be most easily and rapidly enhanced.

Most athletes who work out at Gold's Gym notice a very quick and marked improvement in athletic ability after only a few weeks of weight training. As an example of how quickly these improvements can take place, a woman discus thrower began strength training at Gold's Gym a year ago. At that point, she had a personal record (PR) throw of 121 feet, and she had not come within 5 feet of that PR in eighteen months. After only five months of strength training workouts, however, her PR went up 14 feet, more than she had improved in the three previous years.

Such improvements as this woman made are not uncommon, but individual rates of progress will vary so much that it would be impossible to foretell how much or how fast you will improve. It may be 10 percent or even 30 percent, but the improvement will be dramatic enough to make all the weight training worthwhile.

STRENGTH TRAINING BENEFITS

There are numerous advantages to taking up strength training to improve athletic performance.

Strength Training
Increases Speed

In the preceding section you read that speed is one of the components necessary for maximizing athletic potential. While a certain proportion of movement speed—in sprinting, swinging a bat, skating, twisting, or any other movement—is genetically determined by such inherent factors as bone length, reaction time, and the relative ratio between slow-twitch and fast-twitch muscle fibers (more on this in the next chapter), speed *can* be improved by weight training. And speed combined with strength results in *power*, another key component of athletic performance.

Scientists have found a direct correlation between strength level and speed. One study has shown that those sprinters with very strong thighs and calves are significantly faster in a 40-yard dash than are weaker runners. So if you are a sprinter and you do exercises specifically to improve thigh and calf strength, you will become a faster sprinter than you were before you began using the weights.

Please keep in mind that any speed increases you make through strength training can take place only within the parameters of your genetic ability. You will improve, but all the strength training in the world will not turn a man into an eight-flat 100-meter sprinter or a woman into a nine-flat sprinter over the same distance. (The record for men is 9.95 seconds, for women, 11.0 seconds.) Still, the extra one- or two-tenths improvement in sprint speed can mean the difference between second place and first, or between being tackled at the line of scrimmage and breaking away for the touchdown that wins the game and earns a league title for your team.

Strength Training
Increases Flexibility

It was a common myth in the late 1940s and early 1950s that weight training would make one muscle-bound, or dramatically inflexible. Some of the earliest scientific studies of weight training, which were done as long ago as 1950, refuted this contention and revealed that using weights correctly actually *improves* flexibility.

The champion competitive bodybuilders at Gold's Gym are practical examples of the relationship between weights and flexibility. They train strenuously with weights and have sizable muscles, yet they are among the most flexible of human beings. Almost all of the top men can easily touch their fingers to any point on their backs, and all of them can touch their palms flat on the floor with their legs straight, a feat few "average" individuals can accomplish. If champion bodybuilders can attain and maintain such body flexibility through weight training, so can any athlete.

Strength Training Prevents and/or Reduces Sport Injuries

Football players probably incur more injuries per capita than any other group of athletes, but numerous college and professional football teams have documented dramatic decreases in injury rates among those athletes who have engaged in serious preseason strength workouts.

The part weight training plays in reducing injuries can be vividly seen in the case of a weekend skiing enthusiast. Ski patrol statistics have revealed that most accidents occur late in the day on what was intended to be the last run. With each run the skier becomes more fatigued, and with increased fatigue, less functional strength is available. On the last run, he or she hits a little mogul that might have had no effect earlier in the day, but now the skier is too tired to handle the disruption, loses control, and tears up an ankle or knee. If this same skier had had an excess of strength, the mogul would not have been such a threat. This same principle generalizes to all other sports. Extra strength is an insurance policy against injuries.

In addition to preventing injuries, a couple of strength workouts each week will also help prevent that oh-so-common Monday morning sore muscle syndrome that attacks weekend athletes. If you are a serious weekend athlete, these workouts will also give you a significant edge over most weekenders. You'll run a little faster, jump a little higher, win a little more often, and be none the worse for wear.

Strength Training Maintains Preseason Strength Levels During the Competitive Season

A National Football League study several years ago revealed that athletes who did no weight training during the season lost up to 60 percent of their training-camp (preseason) strength. Those who got in one or two short workouts each week during the competitive season, however, maintained most of their preseason strength levels, and consequently had a higher level of performance than the group that did not weight train.

While it is impossible during the competitive season to participate in weight training sessions that are as long and intense as off-season sessions, light and short workouts will maintain most of your strength. It takes long, hard weight workouts to build appreciable strength, but the experience at Gold's Gym has been that only one to three sets of one exercise for each muscle group, done twice a week with 85 to 90 percent of your preseason exercise poundages (the actual amounts of weight you used in each exercise), will retain approximately 90 to 95 percent of your functional strength over the course of a competitive season.

Strength Training Can Increase, Decrease, or Maintain Body Weight

You can use weight training to gain or lose muscular body weight, or you can significantly increase your strength levels without a body weight gain. You can also maintain your weight over the course of a season, something that is difficult for many individuals. Each of these goals can be attained with the strength training methods described in Chapter 6. Using these methods, a football player or shot putter can gain the weight and strength necessary to reach excellence of performance, and a gymnast or runner can increase strength without adding body weight.

Strength Training Permits a Wide Range of Selectivity in the Exercises

An experienced athlete may reach a sticking point in his or her athletic performance because a single muscle group—or even a segment of a muscle—is too weak for the rest of the body. Like a chain, your athletic ability is only as strong as its weakest link.

In weight training you can choose an exercise that stresses a muscle group or segment of that muscle group, almost in isolation from the rest of the body. For example, an oarsman or oarswoman with a weak lower back can do hyperextensions to strengthen the *erector spinae* muscles, thus eliminating the weak point and quickly improving performance.

This same selectivity of exercise can be used to rehabilitate an injured muscle (covered in more detail in Chapter 4). Briefly, a healed muscle will be significantly weaker than it was before being injured. For this reason, athletic performance will suffer and will return to normal only when the injured muscle group has been fully restored to preinjury strength. By selecting exercises specifically for the injured area, you can speed up this strength rehabilitation process.

Strength Training Allows a Total Range of Resistance

Another advantage of strength training for sports improvement lies in the total range of resistance that is possible with weights. If you have been using calisthenics—pushups, knee bends, and the like—to improve your functional strength, you have doubtless already noticed that you can use only your body weight and no more than that for resistance. And in working at Gold's Gym with individuals who are convalescing from illness, we have observed that some people are too weak to do even the easiest calisthenic movements, because a large part of body weight must be supported in any calisthenic exercise.

Weight training resistance is adjustable. You can load a barbell up to more than 700 pounds and a leg press machine to 1,500, weights that only an infinitesimally small percentage of athletes can use on *any* exercise. Or at the bottom end of this resistance continuum, convalescents have used as little as 2½ pounds in each hand at first. Even the weakest individual, however, will progress rapidly up to the point of using substantial exercise weights.

The Minimal Drawbacks of Strength Training Are Easily Modified

While the advantages of using heavy resistance training far outweigh the disadvantages, there are three drawbacks to consider. Each of these, however, can be minimized by using suggested techniques.

Strength training is repetitious, and you will be doing many of the same exercises thousands of times throughout your athletic career if you choose to weight train. This can lead to boredom, and boredom, to overtraining or less-than-regular workouts.

Despite the repetitious nature of heavy-resistance training, there is much room for variety. The primary way this variety is injected into workouts is by periodically changing the actual training routines. This is usually done each six to eight weeks by substituting equivalent exercises for the ones you have been doing. As an example, you can begin doing bench presses on an incline bench instead of a flat bench.

The second drawback to strength training is that normal weight workouts create only limited cardiorespiratory (heart-lung) fitness. You can, however, use a specialized type of resistance workout called *circuit training* (See Chapter 9.) Circuit training, combining both strength and endurance exercise in one workout, can develop both qualities at the same time quite satisfactorily.

The final drawback to strength training is that even though most athletes doing weight training will merely redistribute their body weight while gaining strength, some will inevitably gain weight. Most athletes lose fat by expending extra calories during weight training at about the same rate they gain muscle. Thus, their body weight remains relatively constant. On the other hand, some athletes have a natural ability to gain muscle tissue. Many Gold's Gym bodybuilders would love to be in this position, but for an athlete in such sports as gymnastics and distance running, a weight gain can spell disaster. For these athletes, a specialized strength-without-weight-increase program is presented in Chapter 6.

A small minority of athletes will gain weight with this special program, even after they have dieted their body fat levels down below 5 percent of the total body weight. This extra weight is, however, functional muscle, which in all likelihood will assist rather than hinder sports performance.

SOME CASE HISTORIES

Numerous athletic teams and individual athletes have achieved national and international championships using strength workouts as an integral part of their overall training plan. In fact, very few athletes these days achieve high competitive levels without strength training, and the following case histories demonstrate how individual athletes and teams have used weights to improve athletic performance.

One of the best-known athletes today is Bruce Jenner, the now-retired 1976 Olympic decathlon gold medalist. For several years before his world-record-breaking performance at Montreal, Jenner did heavy strength training several times a week in the San Jose (California) YMCA weight room.

Bruce Jenner became quite strong from his weight training—eventually becoming capable of bench presses with more than 300 pounds—and this strength translated into progressively better marks, especially in the sprinting and throwing events. Jenner was also able to fully rehabilitate a knee that had been injured and surgically repaired simply by training his legs hard with weights.

A second case of strength training's boosting performance occurred in women's swimming. At the 1976 Olympics, a weight-trained East German team dominated the non-weight-trained American women. A lesson was learned, and the Americans began to use hard weight workouts. By the 1978 World Swimming Championships, the Americans were strong enough to totally turn the tables on the East Germans.

Typical of the American women swimmers is Tracy Caulkins, holder of numerous world records. She has trained hard enough with weights to be able to bench press 140 pounds, which is equal to her own body weight. After the 1972 Olympics, Mark Spitz, winner of seven gold medals that year, was tested on the bench press and could do only 135 pounds, even though his body weight was much higher than Tracy's. This is a good indication of how much champion swimmers have increased their strength levels in only a few years. Spitz didn't have to do weight training in 1972, but if he were swimming now, he would need to lift weights simply to stay even with his competition. Most swimmers are lifting now.

Athletes in both "heavy" and "light" events (those placing maximum or minimum importance on body strength) are using strength training to good advantage. Football is a prototypical "heavy" sport, and every Super Bowl champion team during the 1970s has been weight trained. Typical of these teams is the Pittsburgh Steelers, who do their workouts under the watchful eye of their strength coach, Lou Riecke.

A good example of a "light" sport team using strength training is the Cincinnati Reds baseball team, winner of two consecutive World Series. The Reds place considerable emphasis on off-season strength work, particularly on Nautilus machines at Riverside Stadium. Outfielder George Foster, perennial home run and runs-batted-in champion, is regarded by many as the strongest man in organized baseball. And a former Reds National League Most Valuable Player, infielder Joe Morgan, trains on his own Universal Gym at his home in Oakland, California, during the off-season.

AN OVERVIEW
OF THE GOLD'S GYM
PROGRAM

Virtually all athletes now use strength training in some form. We could cite numerous other case histories of successful strength training for athletic performance, but the point is that strength training does work, and anyone can benefit from strength workouts. In the next chapter, you'll begin learning why and how to strength train by reading about the basic scientific principles underlying strength training. And then in Chapter 3, you'll learn the practical techniques relevant to all weight training.

Chapter 4 tells you how to prevent injuries and rehabilitate injured muscles, knowledge necessary for optimum sports performance. If you master this material, you'll be able to bounce back to peak form following an injury in the shortest possible time.

Chapters 5 through 7 take you through three graduated levels of difficulty in strength training. At each level, you'll learn how to do a variety of exercises and then how to combine these exercises in actual training programs to improve your sports performance. A wide variety of training routines are presented in Chapter 8, each individualized to a specific sport. Chapter 9 teaches you how to gain superendurance or superstrength through weight training. Finally, Chapter 10 deals with the qualifications and duties of a strength coach.

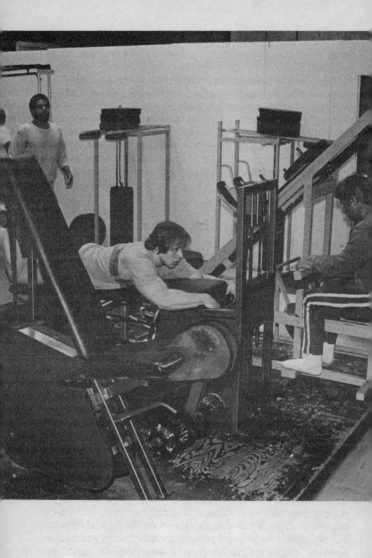

Scientific Strength Training: Muscles and Your Sport

2

Weight training results in direct strength gains, and in the preceding chapter you learned that additional strength results in improved athletic performance. As you will recall, stronger skeletal muscles will allow you to move faster, more precisely, and with greater coordination refinement. Now we will turn to learning how heavy resistance training actually results in strength increases.

Strength training is based on discoveries in the fields of physiology and kinesiology. *Physiology* is the study of all chemical body processes. There are specialists in the field who study only work physiology, or those body processes—such as muscle metabolism, oxygen utilization in muscles, and waste product removal—directly related to muscular work. Because strength training is directly related to muscular work, it is based on principles of exercise physiology, some of which you will learn about in this chapter.

Kinesiology is the analytic study of human movement, the mechanics of how muscles act upon joints. Each exercise you do under the heavy resistance of weight training will be explained in terms of kinesiologic studies on the skeletal muscles. For example, a barball curl puts stress on the biceps and forearm muscles, while a leg extension puts resistance on the quadriceps of the frontal thigh.

The kinesiologists who have studied muscle movement over

the past one hundred years have devised a totally adequate body of exercises aimed at various skeletal muscles. It is the physiologist who is now contributing to advances in strength training, and of this group, the exercise (work) physiologists are most important to weight training.

HOW MUSCLES CONTRACT

One discovery made by exercise physiologists is most fundamental to strength training. It is the physiology of muscle contraction. Without muscle contraction, there would be no body movement, and consequently no strength training.

The bodily components directly responsible for strength are the muscles, and the basic unit of a skeletal muscle is a cylindrically shaped bundle of cells called a *fiber*. Each muscle fiber contains several hundred to several thousand tightly packed cells. The fibers, in turn, are bundled together to form the skeletal muscles. The muscles are attached to the skeleton either directly or by means of tendons.

Muscle Fiber with Cells

When a muscle is working, muscle cells within a fiber exhibit an "all or nothing" phenomenon: They either contract fully or don't contract at all. Generally speaking, larger numbers of cells contract when heavier loads are put on a muscle, but some cells in a muscle fiber will contract during work ("all") and some will not ("nothing"). The degree to which a fiber contracts depends upon the number of cells exhibiting the "all" phenomenon. Some of the fibers in a muscle are maintained in a state of partial contraction known as *muscle tonus*.

Two Kinds of Fibers

There are two types of muscle fibers, each with its own properties and each requiring a specific strength training approach to fully develop it. Fast-twitch fibers give strength and speed to the muscle, and slow-twitch fibers are the endurance component. In general, weight training with very heavy resistance and lower repetitions (in the range of one to five) will enhance fast-twitch development, while training with light weights and very high repetitions (one hundred and over) will strengthen slow-twitch fibers.

Scientists have concluded that, given adequate training, if you have a preponderance of fast-twitch fibers (everyone has a fixed fast-to-slow fiber ratio, ranging from extremes of about 90 percent fast and 10 percent slow to 10 percent fast and 90 percent slow), you would be a natural sprinter and a poor distance runner. And the reciprocal would also be true: Those with mostly slow-twitch fibers are geared toward running marathons, not sprinting.

World class sprinters typically test out at 70 to 80 percent fast-twitch, while quality distance runners have 70 to 80 percent slow-twitch muscle fibers. Frank Shorter, the 1972 Olympic marathon gold medalist, falls into this latter category with 70 percent slow and 30 percent fast.

Determining Your Ratio of Fast- to Slow-Twitch Fibers

By this time a few of you should be at least a little curious to learn what ratios of slow- and fast-twitch fibers you have. A muscle biopsy is the most accurate method of determining this, but by careful observation of a few strength and endurance factors you can gain a relatively clear picture of your fiber ratio. By observing your endurance ability, you can determine fairly accurately your muscle fiber ratio. If you have very little endurance and tremendous speed, your ratio leans toward fast-twitch, while little speed and excellent endurance will put you at the slow-twitch end of the fast/slow continuum. A few individuals will have about equal amounts of speed and endurance, and they fall at the middle of the continuum—about 50/50 fast/slow.

Strength training, especially if you are able to work out in a group, will also give you a good idea of where you stand. The sprinter types will progress very quickly in strength, while the marathoners will move forward more slowly. Those who gain strength most quickly have the highest percentages of fast-twitch fibers.

Regardless of how fast or slow your muscle fibers tend to twitch or of the sport involved, you can dramatically improve your overall strength through heavy-resistance training. And doing so will result in better athletic performance.

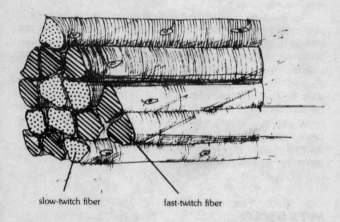

slow-twitch fiber   fast-twitch fiber

Muscle Fiber Distribution

HOW MUSCLES
GROW STRONG

An understanding of muscle contraction is essential to having a clear picture of your body's physiology. Besides complementing this knowledge of muscle contraction, learning about how a muscle increases in size and strength will give you an appreciation of the value of strength training.

The theory of muscle hypertrophy (size and strength growth) now accepted by most physiologists is that the inhibition of catabolism causes the increase in muscle size and strength. In every muscle cell there is a dynamic balance between two kinds of body metabolism: *anabolism* (building up of tissue) and *catabolism* (breaking down of tissue).

In most people, anabolism and catabolism are in equilibrium. Thus, arbitrarily, if an individual has a daily anabolic rate of 25 units, he or she also has a catabolic rate of 25 units. A few individuals are slightly more anabolic or catabolic at times, and either build up tissue or break it down. Anabolic individuals are gaining in muscle size and strength, while catabolic individuals are losing.

By studying the muscle cell *metabolytes* (waste products), physiologists have concluded that anabolism is apparently not increased when one is in an anabolic state due to exercise. Instead, anabolism remains constant, and exercise decreases catabolism, yielding an apparent anabolic effect.

If, in our previous model, we decreased catabolism by 2 units through exercise, it would be at 23 units, while anabolism remained at 25. Then there would be an excess of 2 anabolic units over what there would be in equilibrium. And with 2 extra units of anabolism, the muscle will grow in size and strength, purely as a consequence of the inhibiting effect exercise has on catabolism.

SPECIFICITY

To take full advantage of the physiologic principle that exercise inhibits catabolism, strength exercises must be aimed at specific muscles. Furthermore, to be most effective in adding to your sports performance, the exercises should resemble in kinesiology as closely as possible the actual movements of your sport.

Specificity means a shot putter works out with a heavier-than-usual shot. It means a softball pitcher rigs up a pulley to put resistance on the hand through a pitching motion; a swimmer pulls immobile legs through the water with arm strength alone; an archer uses a heavier-than-normal bow; a place kicker attaches extra weight to his foot; or a sprinter adds ankle weights.

To utilize the concept of specificity of strength training to its fullest potential, you'll have to invent your own exercises to put weight resistance on the proper muscles in close simulation of the movements in your sport. This isn't particularly difficult. Besides using the appropriate workouts in this book, try to match your weight-training movements to the movements of your sport or come up with some of your own exercises.

Repetition Speed

An extension of exercise specificity comes into play in moving a weight very explosively during an exercise. Lightning-quick movements with weights will build more strength and speed into your athletic movements.

The quick movements you do should only be performed toward the end of a group of movements (we call each movement a *repetition*, and each group of repetitions, a *set*). Start out the first two or three repetitions of a set slowly, and then gradually speed up the tempo as the set progresses. Doing so will give your muscles time to warm up and so will prevent injuries. Muscles aren't usually ready for fast movement on the first two to five counts.

Developing the Muscles
for Your Sport

If you plan to use a strength training program specifically tailored to your sport, it is essential to know what muscles are involved. Because it is impossible to develop a full understanding of the relationship between the exercise you do, your skeletal muscles, and your sport without being familiar with the names of the skeletal muscles, we are presenting here anatomical drawings of the major muscles. For each labeled group, we are listing first the commonly used name of the muscle, followed when necessary by the scientific name. All scientific names are in italics.

The best method of finding your sport's muscle groups is to identify those muscles that become sore either after a heavy workout for that sport or from a training session after two or more weeks without training. Because the muscles used the most will become the sorest, this method very accurately identifies the key muscle groups for your sport.

Should the preceding method not appeal to you, you can use the following list to identify the muscle groups involved in the activities that comprise your sport. The names of the muscle groups may at first appear confusing—some are Latin and some are English. The names selected are those in general use, however.

Activity	Muscles Involved
Grasping	All the muscles of the forearms
Throwing	Triceps, forearm flexors, deltoids, *latissimus dorsi*

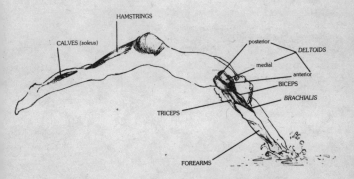

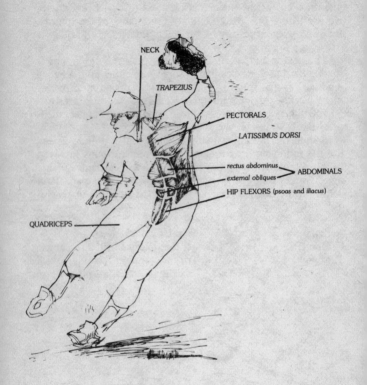

NECK

TRAPEZIUS

PECTORALS

LATISSIMUS DORSI

rectus abdominus   ABDOMINALS
external obliques

HIP FLEXORS (psoas and iliacus)

QUADRICEPS

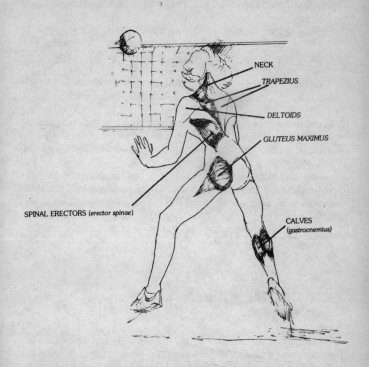

NECK

TRAPEZIUS

DELTOIDS

GLUTEUS MAXIMUS

SPINAL ERECTORS (*erector spinae*)

CALVES
(*gastrocnemius*)

Jumping	Calves, front thighs, gluteals
Running	Front and rear thighs, calves
Pushing objects away from you	Pectorals, deltoids, triceps
Pulling objects to you	*Latissimus dorsi*, biceps, posterior deltoids, forearms
Pulling objects up from the ground	*Trapezius*, deltoids, biceps, forearms
Twisting	Oblique abdominals
Bending	Abdominals, lower back

From these groupings you will know which muscles to stress in strength training. Be sure to include an exercise for each muscle group, and then concentrate your main efforts on the key muscles.

As a further guideline, Chapter 8 has numerous workouts individualized to specific sports. These programs are the end products of analyses such as those just discussed. You'll be able to easily see which muscle groups need to be stressed by observing which body parts are used most in the program for your sport.

STRENGTH/ENDURANCE CONTINUUM

Different sports require varying combinations of strength and endurance, and it's possible to match your strength training to duplicate the combination needed for your sport. With weight training you can gain superior strength, superior endurance, or combinations of the two, but not both super strength and super endurance at the same time. This is because endurance and strength are somewhat mutually exclusive qualities. If you have a large percentage of one, the percentage of the other will be relatively small. Keep in mind that these percentages are relative. While some individuals in superior physical condition appear to have a combination of superstrength and superendurance, in actuality they could attain vastly higher levels of one or the other through specialized development.

YOU'RE THE EXPERT

Regardless of the advice you get in this book, you remain the expert on your body. You're the only one who can feel how your body responds. You're the one who can digest all the information you can find on strength training and use it to develop an intuitive feel for what works best on and in your body.

By getting in touch with your body, you'll be able to adapt the information in this book to suit your needs. Monitor your energy levels, strength gain rates, fatigue buildup rates, flexibility, mental attitude, mood, pulse rate, the feel of your body moving under resistance. Try to relate each of these factors to how you are progressing in your sport, and you will develop a natural aptitude for training which will enable you to progress more rapidly.

Tips and
Techniques
for Effective
Strength Training

3

There is much more to strength training than merely pulling on a barbell or pushing on a weight machine. For maximum effectiveness, strength training should be approached systematically. This chapter will acquaint you with the facts about equipment and technique you'll need to know for your first heavy-resistance workout.

EQUIPMENT

In strength training, your tools of the trade will be conventional free weights (barbells, dumbbells, and the various pulley systems, benches, and racks associated with them), the Universal Gym and similar machines, and Nautilus machines, either by themselves or in various combinations of machines and free weights. All are effective, but each offers unique advantages and disadvantages.

Free Weights

Free weights include barbells, dumbbells, and related equipment that is differentiated from such exercise machines as Uni-

versal Gyms or Nautilus. Barbells and dumbbells have been in existence for more than a century. Barbells are long bars with adjustable weights attached to each end. They are used singly and are held with both hands. Dumbbells are shortened versions of a barbell (usually not more than a foot in length, as opposed to the five- or six-foot barbells) which are used as pairs, one in each hand. At first barbells and dumbbells were thick bars with clumsy iron globes permanently attached to each end. Each barbell or dumbbell was limited to a single fixed poundage. Later the globes were made hollow and openings were provided in each so that lead shot could be added or removed, a crude method for adjusting the weight.

In 1902, Allan Calvert invented the weighted disk version still in general use. Seventy-five years of improvements have only slightly altered his design, and there is little difference between Calvert's adjustable barbell and the ones you will find in Gold's Gym today. In addition, many large organized gyms like Gold's provide a full range of barbells and dumbbells with weights welded permanently in place. These "fixed weights" are a little more convenient than adjustable sets because no time is required to change weights.

While barbell and dumbbell design has remained essentially the same, substantial advances in conventional weight training have been brought about by the addition of various benches, pulleys, and racks designed to take full advantage of the downward pull of gravity. Through the combined use of all weight-

Decline Bench　　　**Flat Bench**　　　**Incline Bench**

Lat Machine

related equipment, it is now possible to isolate resistance not only to a single muscle group, but also to different parts of each group.

Benches have been built to place the body at various angles along a 180-degree arc from perfectly upright to head down in order to work with or against the downward pull of gravity. A variety of pulley arrangements has also been devised to circumvent gravity. The most common pulley device is known as a lat machine. It has a bar that can be pulled down from overhead to the neck in the same manner you would chin up to a horizontal bar. This pulley is particularly useful if athletes are not strong enough to lift their body weight for chin-ups, because a lighter weight can be used over the same range of motion.

Squat Rack

One commonly used rack is the squat rack. It consists of a pair of stands that can cradle a heavy weight at shoulder height. This rack comes in handy when doing deep knee bends with a barbell behind your neck. Can you imagine how hard it would be to get 300 pounds behind your neck using only your arms?

Free weights offer three major advantages. First, they really are *free*, that is, they allow you to use your body fully. No machine can help you catch a ball, run, change directions, accelerate explosively, or fly through the air with total body control. *You* control your body in your sport, so *you* should control the resistance you use in strength training. It seems likely that, if you control the weight you use in exercising, you will have better control over the strength you build.

The second advantage has to do with the money you save training with free weights. If you *buy* equipment for a well-equipped gym, the free weights and related equipment you need for a total workout will cost you between $500 and $1000. A Universal Gym to work the whole body can cost $2500, and a Nautilus machine, the same or more to train *one body part*. If you join a weight club, a typical cost is $200 a year, the same as you'd pay to train at Gold's Gym. The cheapest Nautilus facility membership costs 50 percent more.

The final advantage of free weights lies in the adage, "Variety is the spice of life." Free weights offer variety, and machines don't. Universal Gyms and Nautilus machines might each have as many as three exercises to choose from for each body part. Give us an hour or so, and we can come up with one hundred free-weight movements for every muscle group. That's variety, and variety means less chance of boredom.

Along with the good walks the bad, and there are two disadvantages to using conventional weight training equipment. The first is the other side of the initial advantage we noted: the weights are free, so some athletes find it difficult to control them during initial workouts. If this frustrates you, you might try Universal or Nautilus. Otherwise, take solace in the fact that you'll have more control soon, not only over the weights, but over yourself.

The second disadvantage is the only one we give any credence to: machines are safer, because they have been constructed with safety features that keep you from being pinned under a weight. You don't have this problem with dumbbells, and trained spotters ensure that you won't have this problem with barbells. If you get stuck, they can lift a barbell off you. Otherwise, an archaeologist might find your skeleton 500 years from now in the ruins of a gym pinned beneath a rusty 400-pound barbell!

Actually, it's not quite that bad. Later in this chapter, we'll explain the accepted safety procedures to you. They will make free weights almost as safe as the machines, but you need to train with a partner when pumping really heavy iron.

Universal Gym

Universal Gyms

Universal Gyms have really caught on the past few years, especially in schools, YMCAs, and other high-use facilities. We have one at Gold's Gym, and it's in almost constant use.

The primary advantage of a Universal machine is its versatility in group situations. As many as ten athletes can be on a single machine at one time, because it has various exercise stations. The resistance can be changed extremely quickly with movable pins in each weight stack. With the multiple stations and weight selection features, each Universal Gym can accommodate groups of fifteen to twenty athletes at a time. Two can share each station with one resting while the other exercises.

Another advantage of the Universal Gym is the control factor we've talked about. The resistance at each exercise station is designed to be moved along a predetermined arc, which is totally controlled by the machine. For some this is an advantage, but we've already pointed out that it can be a disadvantage as well.

We've also touched on the primary disadvantage: cost. Even used Universal machines are going for $1,500 each, at least twice what a set of free weights and related equipment to perform the same functions would cost. And unlike barbells, Universal and similar machines require frequent maintenance.

The main disadvantage of Universal Gyms and other comparable machines lies, as we've said, in the lack of variety of exercises. Universal provides only one or two per muscle group. Because strength training is repetitious, limiting the number of exercises increases boredom. And boredom is the last thing an athlete needs!

Nautilus Machines

The Nautilus machine is a child of the seventies, and such machines have come into common use with athletic teams. There are approximately twenty different kinds of these machines. Some have only one function; others two. Gold's Gym

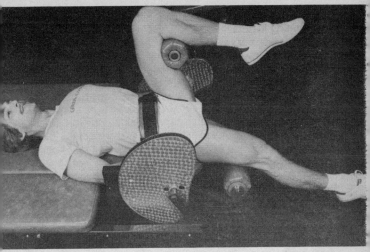

Nautilus Machine

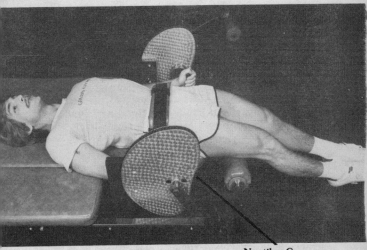

Nautilus Cam

has several such machines, and two or three of them are used frequently.

As conceived by inventor Arthur Jones, Nautilus machines offer near-perfect exercise. They've conquered gravity by using rotary cams (pulleys) to place the pull of gravity exactly opposite at all times to the path you are pulling or pushing along, a feature few free-weight or Universal exercises can match.

Nautilus machines also offer resistance along a full range of motion for each muscle group, a feature also not found in Universal Gyms or with free weights. This is a distinct advantage, because a muscle developed over its full movement range will be significantly stronger than one accustomed to resistance over less than its full range.

The final advantage Nautilus has over its competitors is balanced resistance, The cam, or pulley, of each Nautilus machine is computer-designed to have varying radii, and these varying radii are *balanced* to the natural strength levels of the muscle along the range of its movement. Because the resistance feels heavier when the radius is shorter, the Nautilus design employs shorter radii to put the most resistance at the contracted position of a muscle, where the most muscle fibers are flexing and where the most weight should logically be placed on a muscle. Balanced resistance is a tremendous advance over conventional weights, which place maximum resistance predominantly in the middle range of motion, where the muscle is weaker than at the start or finish of a movement.

By combining full rotary movement and balanced resistance, Nautilus machines make it possible to thoroughly exhaust a muscle in 50 percent, or even as little as 25 percent, of the total time it would take to do so with Universal Gyms or free weights. This, to say the least, is a tremendous advance in strength training, but it costs.

The expense of Nautilus machines is prohibitive for private individuals. We estimate a $30,000 equipment outlay to be necessary if you want to work your entire body. To have a full Nautilus installation would cost even more. A $300 to $400 Nautilus facility annual membership fee is still within range for most athletes, however.

The other disadvantage—a familiar one at this point—is the limited number of exercises you can do for each muscle group. For example, there are only two (leg extension and leg press) for the frontal thigh, as opposed to scores for that area with free weights. So you will have to balance the possibility of boredom against the ultimate benefits of Nautilus machine exercise.

WHERE TO WORK OUT

There are literally thousands of places to do strength workouts. If you live in greater Los Angeles, we'd like to see you at Gold's Gym, but there are other suitable strength-training facilities elsewhere.

Nautilus locations are cropping up in every fair-sized metropolis. If you can afford the expense, you'll find them more than adequate places in which to develop your body power. They are better than all the health clubs around the world, because they actually cater to athletic training. Health spas are even more expensive than Nautilus gyms, and they are chrome-platedly inadequate for any type of heavy athletic training.

Other possibilities to consider are a YMCA or YWCA, school facility, or your garage. The first two can vary widely in quantity of equipment, and any sort of institutionalized gym leaves you at the mercy of a clock. If you get off work at 10:00 P.M. and the Y closes at 9:00, you may be forced to use boulders for barbells. If you find a school or Y weight room that's well equipped and open when you need it, however, such a facility will be ideal for hard athletic workouts.

If none of the aforementioned alternatives is available to you, or if you prefer privacy, open your own home gym. The cost of setting up a garage or basement gym is a one-time expense, compared to yearly dues at a club or other facility. The primary advantage of a home gym is convenience, the chance to do some bench presses at 4:00 in the morning if you want to. The main disadvantage, however, is the lack of comradeship. Having training partners increases enthusiasm and training drive. Without someone to push you, or against whose record you can compare your progress, you may never reach your maximum rate of strength improvement.

You can considerably reduce the initial cost of setting up your home gym by using your ingenuity. Look or advertise for used equipment. Many people start weight training with brand-new equipment, then decide not to continue. After two weeks, the barbells and benches are consigned to the attic. You can get those unused pieces for a 50 to 75 percent discount. People will be clamoring to sell, so you can be selective and choose only the metal weights. Vinyl and concrete plates are too thick to fit any substantial poundage on a bar.

For the benches and racks, any carpentry skill you have can be combined with boards and nails to build some very serviceable pieces of equipment. If you don't know one end of a saw from another, find someone who does and offer to exchange free workouts in your new gym for some light construction. It works every time.

HOW TO LEARN
THE ROPES—
OR WEIGHTS

This book is one of your best sources of information on strength training, but any book leaves some room for error. Reading books simply isn't the same as being there in person. Your best bet for reliable information is a combination of what you're holding in your hands and the athletes you train with. We can give you an appreciation of all the techniques and exercises you'll need to know, and your friends can check out your form in the weight room. As time goes on, you and your friends can exchange experiences and gradually evolve the individualized training programs that will get the job done best for you.

DEFINITIONS

Before we go any farther, a few basic definitions will help you better understand what is going on in the weight room.

An *exercise* is whatever strength training movement you are doing. An exercise can be a free-hand knee bend, or its barbell equivalent, the squat. We sometimes use the word *movement* to mean an exercise.

Each individual time you do an exercise, let's say each time you do a push-up or bench press, you are doing a *repetition*. Often you'll hear this referred to as a *rep*.

If you do a group of repetitions, eight or ten or fifty or whatever, you've done a set. Usually multiple sets are done of each exercise in your *training routine*, which is also called a *schedule* or *program*. Between each set are rest periods called *intervals*. Intervals are simply rests between efforts at an exercise.

TIME FACTORS: HOW OFTEN AND WHEN

After you've thoroughly exercised a muscle, it is necessary to rest it for approximately forty-eight hours before you work it again. For this reason, athletes usually have a rest day between workout days. A muscle group should be exercised on three nonconsecutive days each week, for example, Monday, Wednesday, and Friday; Sunday, Tuesday, and Thursday; or whatever other convenient combination you can come up with. Later we'll talk about training on what's called a split routine, wherein you can work out four to six days a week by exercising half of your body one day and letting it rest the next while you train the other half. For now, however, plan on training your whole body on three nonconsecutive days each week.

Your strength workout can be at any time during the day, but it is best to have it at least two or three hours before or after your sports activity. Heavy work causes slight blood congestion in the muscles, because heavier-than-normal circulation is necessary to remove fatigue toxins in the muscle and replace them with new fuel stores. This congestion is the famous "pump" the bodybuilders talk about so reverently. It lasts only an hour or two, but it does have a temporary tightening effect on the muscles, which can lessen muscle control. If you play basketball immediately after weight training, for example, your shooting touch will be off a little. It's better, then, to wait a couple of hours for the pump to subside.

A final time factor in strength training is the length of the

39

rest periods or intervals between sets. If you don't rest enough, you won't have your strength back for the next set. If you rest too much, you begin to cool off, which increases the risk of injury. Experience has shown that a 60- to 90-second rest interval is best, so you should try to stay in that range when training.

PHYSICAL EXAMINATIONS

At every level of scholastic sports participation, a physical examination is required, so many of you readers can skip our warnings. If you are participating in any sort of athletics *without* a physical, you are taking your life in your hands, especially if you are over forty. If you haven't had a physical recently, get one. If at all possible, insist that a stress test EKG (electrocardiogram) be part of your exam. Some cardiac irregularities show up only under the exercise of this stress test. Most authorities suggest such a test for persons over forty. We recommend one for serious athletes in any age group.

THE WORKOUT

Warming Up

In many ways strength training will be more difficult than anything physical you've ever done. Because the work load is so heavy, we strongly suggest that you warm up before doing any heavy-resistance work. Physiologists have determined that a good warm-up before any physical activity has three primary values: (1) it prevents injuries; (2) it refines movement skills so that you won't be clumsy; and (3) it makes muscles more efficient. We recommend approximately 5 to 10 minutes of continuous calisthenics and stretching, alternating the two every 2 or 3 minutes. Finish this off with one set of fifteen reps on each exercise with a weight no more than 40 percent of what you intend to use as your maximum exercise poundage each workout. Doing a light set on each movement as you come to it will finish your warm-up for each individual exercise.

There are two main things to keep in mind when warming up before a strength workout. First, keep up a steady pace, resting only 15 to 30 seconds between exercises. Doing so will gradually accelerate your pulse rate and warm up your muscles and joints. Second, never bounce while stretching. Ease toward the point of maximum extension, where you feel mild pain in the muscle being exercised, and hold that position for a few seconds before returning to the starting position. Bouncing into stretches activates what is called the stretch reflex mechanism. Once activated, this mechanism limits the range of any stretch to something shorter than can be achieved by easing into stretching positions. So don't bounce.

Warm-up Routine

A good routine for warming up would be:

1. Jumping Jacks: about 50 to 100 repetitions
2. Lower Back/Hamstring Stretch: about 60 to 90 seconds to each side
3. Push-Ups: 20 to 50 repetitions
4. Towel Stretch (for shoulders): 60 to 90 seconds to each side
5. Free-Hand Squats: 25 to 50 repetitions
6. *Latissimus Dorsi* Stretch: 60 to 90 seconds to each side
7. Calf Stretch: 60 to 90 seconds for each calf
8. Crossed-Legs Lower Back/Hamstring Stretch: 60 to 90 seconds to each side

Many books dealing with warm-ups are available. If you would prefer some warm-up routine other than the one detailed here, Hyman Jampol's *The Weekend Athlete's Way to a Pain-Free Monday* and Bob Anderson's *Stretching* present some alternatives (see Suggested Reading).

Warm-Up Exercises

JUMPING JACKS

Jumping jacks are a good general body exercise to begin warming up with.

Starting Position

Stand erect with your feet about twelve inches apart and your arms down at your sides.

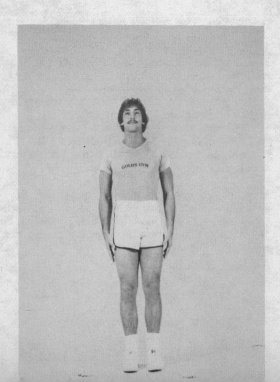

Performance

Jump up off the ground about six inches. As you jump, swing your arms straight out to your sides and then up until your hands touch directly overhead and spread your legs so that your feet land about two to three feet apart. As soon as your feet hit (they should reach the floor at the same time your hands touch overhead), bounce back up six inches and simultaneously return your arms and legs to the starting position. You will soon develop a bouncy rhythm with no stops anywhere in the movement.

LOWER BACK/
HAMSTRING STRETCH

This stretching movement will begin to loosen up your *erector spinae* muscles and the hamstrings at the backs of your thighs.

Starting Position

Spread your legs two to three feet apart and lock your knees so your legs stay straight throughout the movement. Standing erect in this position, spread your arms straight out to the sides at shoulder height.

Performance

From this position, twist down and to the left to touch your right hand to your left instep. Return to the starting position and repeat to the opposite side, touching your left hand to your right foot. Alternate sides at a steady cadence for 60 to 90 seconds for each side.

PUSH-UPS

This old stand-by calisthenic exercise will warm up your entire upper body, but especially your pectorals, deltoids, and triceps.

Starting Position

Assume a position with your toes and hands on the floor. Your toes should be as far apart as is comfortable for you. Your hands should be at shoulder width apart, fingers forward, below your chest. Extend your body and lock it straight. Do not allow your stomach or lower back to sag.

Performance

From this starting position, bend your arms and let your body sink until your chest touches the floor. Push back up to the starting point and repeat 20 to 50 times.

TOWEL STRETCH

By stretching your shoulders with a towel or piece of rope, you can keep that part of your body supple and prepare your shoulders for such heavy exercises as bench presses and military presses.

Starting Position

With your palms facing your thighs, grasp a towel or rope in front of your thighs such that the distance between your hands is two feet greater than that between your shoulders. Lift your arms straight overhead and spread them as far apart as the towel or rope will allow.

Performance

From this starting position, move your right arm out and down to the side until your upper left arm is straight up and your biceps rest against your left ear. Move your right arm backward until your shoulder dislocates down and backward. Keep your arms straight throughout the movement. Follow the right shoulder with a dislocate of the left so both arms are behind your back, palms up. Dislocate both shoulders back up to the starting position, the right one first, and repeat to the opposite side.

Note: As your shoulders become more supple, you can gradually reduce the distance between your hands on the towel or rope. Once you can dislocate both sides in each direction with your hands at shoulder width or narrower, you will have superior shoulder flexibility.

FREE-HAND SQUATS

The calisthenic counterpart of the strength training squat will warm up all of your leg muscles for heavier work with squats and leg presses.

Starting Position

Stand erect with your hands on your hips and your feet about one shoulder width apart, toes pointed slightly outward.

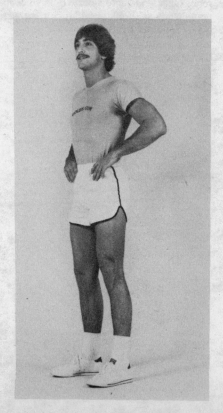

Performance

Slowly bend your knees and sink down into a deep knee bend until your thighs are parallel to the floor. Return to the starting position and repeat 25 to 50 times.

LATISSIMUS DORSI
STRETCH

This movement will stretch out all of your upper back muscles, but especially the *latissimus dorsi*.

Starting Position

Stand about eighteen inches away from any handy upright pole or bar. (One of the long corner members of a Universal Gym will do nicely, or you can simply hang onto both sides of a door handle.) Grasp the bar or pole at shoulder level with your fingers interlaced. Bend your knees and sink toward the floor until your spine slopes downward at approximately a 45-degree angle to the floor from shoulders to hips. Force your hips back away from the grip point to stretch your *latissimus dorsi*.

Performance

From this position pull yourself toward the bar with *latissimus* and biceps strength until your forehead touches the bar or pole. Return to the stretched position, trying to stretch the upper back more with each repetition, and repeat for the required length of time.

CALF STRETCH

After any sort of running or jogging, it is a good idea to stretch your calves.

Starting Position

Stand next to and facing a wall with your feet about one shoulder width apart. Place your hands about one shoulder width apart on the wall directly in front of your chest. Simultaneously "walk" your arms down the wall and your feet away from the wall, keeping your entire body straight, until your body slopes down at a 45-degree angle from head to feet. You will be up on your toes.

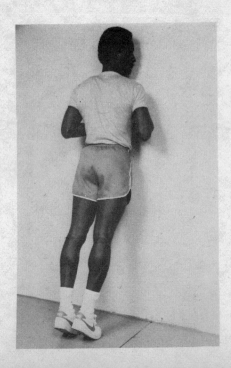

Performance

Moving only your ankle joints, try to gradually force your heels down to the floor while keeping your knees locked and your body stiff. After each downward stretch, rise up on your toes and stretch down again. Start by stretching both feet together. After 30 to 60 seconds, stretch one leg at a time, alternating between the two.

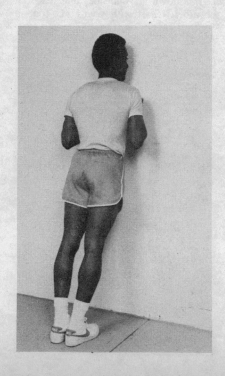

CROSSED-LEGS LOWER BACK/ HAMSTRING STRETCH

This exercise is somewhat more difficult to do than the first Lower Back/Hamstring Stretch in this routine, so it is placed at the end of the stretching program when you are more warmed up and your muscles are better prepared for severe stretches. It will give you a good final lower back and hamstring stretch.

Starting Position

Stand erect with your arms down at your sides and one foot crossed in front of the other. (Start with your right foot in front.)

Performance

Bend over at your waist, keeping your legs straight, and try to touch your hands to your toes or even to the floor in front of your forward foot. This will stretch both hamstrings, but especially the muscles along the back of your front leg. Return to the starting position. Do a total of about ten stretches before changing to put your left foot in front. After ten stretches with your left foot in front, switch back to having your right foot in front. Alternate feet until you have done stretches to each side for 60 to 90 seconds.

Sore Muscles

There's no way to avoid sore muscles after your first few strength workouts. It's a natural occurrence because your body just isn't ready for heavier-than-usual exercise. Your muscles aren't used to the stress, especially not over a full range of motion, and your body's not prepared to work at removing the larger-than-usual amount of fatigue waste products. So you get sore.

Your consolation is that the body is a marvelously adaptable machine. It very quickly becomes accustomed to new exercises and won't become sore again unless you make another dramatic increase in the work load you are placing on certain muscles.

To minimize muscle soreness, we suggest a slow break-in and very light initial exercise weights. When you look over the training programs later in this book, *don't* be tempted to do the entire workout during your first exercise session. Just do one set of each movement the first time or two. Then gradually add weight and sets until you are up to the full workout.

If you do get violently sore, the only reliable relief is a long, hot bath, preferably with several tons of epsom salts thrown in. Other possible, but less reliable, remedies include massage and increased doses of vitamin C.

Strict Form

You will end up stronger if you exercise each muscle along its full range of movement, taking care to extend every muscle to its maximum and then to flex it thoroughly. Thus, to get the full benefits from weight training, you should raise and lower the weight in a slow and deliberate manner on each repetition. Swinging or "cheating" the weight up will cause you to neglect some segment of the full movement. On the other hand, lowering the weight under control will make the downward arc of your movement as valuable to your strength development as the upward segment.

Breathing

Trying to decide how to breathe during strength training can literally take your breath away. There are authorities who will tell you to breathe in as the weight is raised and out as it is lowered. Others say just the opposite. We've given each of these methods a fair trial at Gold's Gym and have finally concluded that it makes little difference when one breathes. Try each method and settle on the one that is most comfortable for you. Or, just breathe whenever it becomes necessary.

Safety Procedures

Strict observance of two common safety procedures would eliminate 99 percent or more of all training injuries. The first such procedure is checking to see that all the collars (the fas-

Barbell Collar

tening devices on the outer ends of barbells and dumbbells that hold the plates in position) are in place and tightened. With limit weights, one end of a barbell will invariably go up faster than the other. If the collars are not in place or have not been tightened, the plates will slide off the lower end, and you will severely injure your back when the heavy side whips down.

The second safety procedure is to have a spotter or two watching carefully when you use maximum poundages. Be especially sure to have one at the head of your bench when doing bench presses. The only known strength-training death occurred to a man benching alone. He lost control of a heavy barbell, which crashed down across his throat.

Training Partners

The best way to be sure of a spotter is to train regularly with someone. Training partners come in handy in other ways, too. You'll be less tempted to miss a workout, for example, if you know someone is waiting for you at the gym. And the natural rivalry that develops between partners leads to more dynamic workouts.

When choosing a partner, look for someone who is willing to follow the program you're on. Ideally he or she should be in your sport and at your approximate ability level. It will be more convenient if your partner is as strong as you are because you'll need to change weights less often. The final requirement is that the partner be dependable. *You* don't want to be left waiting at the gym.

Once you have a good training partner, use him or her to your advantage. By jumping in on exercises as fast as your partner finishes, you can speed up your workouts, which builds better cardiorespiratory fitness. And with a regular spotter, you'll be able to force up your exercise poundages without fear of being stuck under heavier-than-normal weight.

Overtraining:
Causes and Solutions

Your body's energy reserves are much like the amount of money you have in your checking account. If you keep taking energy out without putting some back in, you're going to go broke. We call this going broke "over-training," and it can be as big a disaster as overdrawing at the bank.

The only good way you can deposit energy is through proper sleep and rest, a good diet, and workouts within your capacity. Work out too long or lose too much sleep, and before you know it, you've overtrained.

You'll definitely know when you've gone too far into energy debt because you will suddenly lose all interest in ever again touching a weight. You'll also feel tired all of the time, and if you keep a record of it, your pulse rate will gradually go up. You might even experience a mild case of insomnia or a loss of appetite.

The only way to kill overtraining before it kills you is to reverse the trend toward an energy deficit. Start by taking a few days off: Don't train in the weight room or participate in your sport. Follow this break with shorter workouts, more sleep, a better diet, and maybe a total change of workout routine.

Once your energy balance is back to normal, you can take a few precautions that'll lower the chances of overtraining again. Be regular in your diet and sleep, and be sure to progress slowly in the total number of sets you do during each workout. You can train as hard as you want, but keep the length of your workouts down.

Sleep

It's been said that each twenty-four hours is divided into three equal segments. The first eight hours are for sleep; the second eight, for work; and the third, for recreation. This is not true for athletes.

If you're an athlete with a regular job, you're actually

"working" *more* than eight hours when you add in your training time, so it stands to reason that you'll need more sleep than the average person. As a general rule, we recommend that athletes sleep between eight and nine hours a day, although we have observed athletes who actually need up to twelve hours of sleep each day. Try sleeping eight or more hours at night and taking a short nap in the late afternoon. If you can't nap, at least lie down and rest yourself physically. It'll recharge your batteries for the rest of the day, and will help prevent overtraining.

Progression

The very heart of weight training for athletic strength, the foundation upon which the entire activity is based, is progressive increases of resistance. The body reacts to an overload by adapting to it, and this adaptation comes in the form of strength increase.

As an example of progression, let's consider your body as capable of producing 100 arbitrary units of strength on a regular basis. If we subjected it to a load of 102 units, the load would feel heavy to you, but it would force your muscles to adapt so that they would be able to handle 102 units regularly instead of the original 100. Without the regular 2-unit increase in resistance, however, you would remain at the ability level necessary to handle 100 units.

The reason for the body's remaining at this same level and for its adapting lies in the concept of equilibrium. An equilibrium exists between the strength of your muscles and the demands you regularly place on them. If the stress on muscles is more or less constant, they will remain at a level of strength adequate to this stress. Most manual laborers do great amounts of physical work each day, but very few of them develop tremendous strength because their work load remains relatively constant.

There is an equilibrium between work demands and muscle output. To overcome this equilibrium, it is necessary to increase progressively the work loads in a strength workout. In our example, your muscles will adapt to accommodate 103 units if you demand a strength increase by placing 103 units of stress on them. And once you are used to 103 units, you must immediately begin to use 104. By constantly increasing the resistance, you will make your muscles become progressively stronger.

Thus, it is only through progressively applied resistance increases that the muscles continue to grow in strength. To achieve these increases in strength training, we (1) increase the reps, sets, or poundages used; (2) cut the rest intervals; or (3) both. In actual practice, the rest intervals are usually held constant at 60 to 90 seconds, and the reps, sets, and exercise weights are adjusted.

For example, if we start a bench press exercise at 50 pounds for 8 reps, the next workout will be 50 pounds for 9 reps. In successive workouts, we will add one or more repetitions per set up to 12 reps. At this point, the weight is increased by 5 pounds, and we start back at 8 reps using a 55-pound weight. Then the reps are again brought up to 12, the weight is increased to 60 pounds and the reps, cut to 8.

You will probably find you can add more than one rep per workout. You shouldn't be afraid to progress too fast on your exercise poundage, so push for as many new reps each workout as possible.

As you progress in your strength training, you might be doing a program with more than one set per exercise. If so, you will be trying to add one repetition or more to each set. And you should never add weight to the multiple sets until you reach the required number of reps on all the sets.

The range of reps you'll be given for programs in later chapters (e.g., 80 pounds for 10 to 15 reps) are called *guide numbers*. In this example, 10 is the lower guide number, the minimum number of repetitions you should reach for each set. The upper guide number is 15, so you'll be working out for between 10 and 15 reps each set. Keep in mind that as part of the progression you'll be asked to do different rep ranges for different exercises, so stay alert to these guide numbers.

Individualizing
Your Strength Training

At this point we must caution against doggedly sticking to a training schedule just because we've recommended it somewhere in this book. Each athlete involved in strength training should experiment with new routines, equipment, and techniques to find the ideal personalized weight training program.

When experimenting, be sure to give your program a six- to eight-week trial. This will give you a chance to see if it works. Keep mental or written notes of the effects you achieve with different exercises and combinations of exercises. Be careful, however, not to remain on a routine more than six to eight weeks at a time, because doing so will lead to boredom and overtraining.

When it's time to change routines, pick a new one from a later chapter or begin to individualize. If you like the program you're on and are still making progress with it, adapt it by substituting new exercises for similar ones in your present routine. For example, you might substitute incline presses for bench presses, or squats for leg presses.

Training Diary

The ultimate method of gauging your body's reactions is to keep a training diary. Enter the date, the exercises done, and the weight, sets, and reps for each movement. You may also wish to include the time of day, your attitude, your pulse rates, the elapsed time for each workout, and so on. Actually, any data you can include may prove helpful a few months or years from now. From such data you can easily see exactly how you have reacted to the different exercises, routines, and techniques with which you have experimented over a period of time.

Several recording codes exist for noting the weight, sets, and reps of an exercise. Below are several ways of saying 100 pounds for three sets of 10 reps:

100/3 × 10
100 × 10 × 10 × 10
100/3/10
3 × 10:100

Any of these methods is acceptable if you can understand a year from now what you wrote down today.

Correct Level

Each person who picks up this book should begin strength training at the correct level. If you are a beginner, there's no problem, because you can open the book to the first page and progress straight through. If you have had some strength training, however, you will need some guidelines on where to begin again.

If you can remember the last time you did some strength work and can recall approximately how many total sets you did each workout, it will be easy to give you a good general guideline for your reentry level. Should you have been off six months or less, do 50 percent of the total number of sets you used to do for your first workout, and use a poundage approximately 50 percent less than you used to handle in each movement. If you've been off more than six months, try a 33/33 formula instead of 50/50. Either way, work up slowly in both sets and poundages from this beginning point.

If you can't remember your sets and poundages and you've done three months or less of weight workouts, pretend you're a beginner and go in at Level One (Chapter 5). If you've had three to six months of weight workouts, begin at Level Two (Chapter 6). And if you have more than six months of experience, you know enough about your body to make your own decisions.

Injuries: Prevention and Rehabilitation

4

Injuries are the bane of any athlete's existence, and they seem to go hand in hand with athletics. Injuries can occur at any time and often for no apparent reason. They occur occasionally in strength training, but with proper precautions they can be almost completely avoided.

In this short chapter we will explore types of injuries. We will see how strength training injuries will be avoided and how any injury can be given first aid. Finally, we will learn how to use strength workouts to fully rehabilitate injured joints and muscles.

TYPES OF INJURIES

The least severe kinds of sports injuries are *abrasions* (scratches and scrapes) and *contusions* (bruises). Both are uncommon in strength training and occur only when someone is careless enough to drop a loose plate on his or her foot. They are far more common in contact sports such as football, field hockey, ice hockey, and boxing. Because strength training will not prevent or heal abrasions and contusions, the only strength-training consideration in regard to such injuries is that it is sometimes difficult to strength train a bruised muscle. Treat bruised muscles carefully, tempering your exercise whenever you feel more than a slight pain. The weights you use to exercise bruised muscles can be quite light without allowing muscle strength to diminish. Once a muscle has been strengthened, even small amounts of low-intensity exercise will maintain high degrees of strength and tone.

Muscle *stretches* (usually called strains) and *tears* (called pulls) are more serious injuries. The mildest form of these is the muscle soreness you get following any new and strenuous physical activity. Such strains can vary in severity but are usually minor and merely involve greater-than-normal stretching of individual muscle fibers.

Muscle pulls are slightly worse and involve actual tearing of muscle tissues, from a few strands up to a severe parting of a complete muscle group. Gymnasts are very susceptible to biceps tears when doing ring work, for example. Sprinters, who subject their hamstrings to enormous stresses, are very likely to pull muscles in that area.

Occasionally, the muscle itself will withstand extremely heavy stresses, but the tendons attaching the muscle to the bone will tear. The most common example of such ruptures occurs in the Achilles tendon leading from the lower end of the calf to the heel. There have been numerous widely publicized cases of Achilles tendon ruptures among professional athletes in recent years.

Strains are fairly common in strength training. In fact, they are the most typical weight-related injury, while actual tears are rare and usually occur only in competitive Olympic-style weightlifting, which involves quick movements under heavy loads.

Bone breaks can be very serious injuries. A few fractures are caused by stress buildups, such as those brought on by running long distances or playing basketball or tennis on concrete courts. Such stress fractures are fairly minor injuries which heal quickly with rest from the activity that caused them.

Traumatic bone breaks, on the other hand, must be put in a cast to heal. And during six weeks of plaster and inactivity, the muscles around a joint atrophy dramatically and lose strength. While strength training won't heal a fracture, it will very quickly restore size and strength to atrophied muscle tissue.

The most debilitating injury is a joint displacement. This

is commonly a dislocation or a cartilage or ligament tear. Rest and gradual strength rehabilitation will usually restore a dislocated joint to its former condition. Cartilage and ligament damage, however, require corrective surgery, casting, and eventual muscular rehabilitation.

CAUSES OF STRENGTH-TRAINING INJURIES

Most strength-training injuries are caused by not warming up or by poor biomechanical positioning, that is, bad body form while lifting. Injuries can be prevented by warming up thoroughly (see Chapter 3), maintaining a steady training pace (resting no more than 60 to 90 seconds between sets), and practicing proper biomechanics. As exercises are explained in the next three chapters, such mechanics will be emphasized. Noting these biomechanical tips carefully and putting them into practice will help you avoid strength-training injuries.

FIRST AID

If you are inattentive or unlucky enough to be injured while weight training, immediate first aid is essential to control the severity of the injury. For both muscle and joint injuries, apply ice. Put an ice pack or block of ice directly on the injury for five minutes at a time as often as you can stand it. The ice limits swelling, an essential factor for quick recovery from injuries, and it often prevents a muscle from cramping and doing additional damage to itself. See your physician as soon as possible for a diagnosis of the severity of the injury. He or she will recommend rehabilitation procedures, which typically begin with two or three days of rest and periodic heat applications to promote healing.

REHABILITATION
AFTER INJURY

Once the physician gives you a go-ahead to resume light weight work, you'll be well on your way to full recovery. Start out with the lightest possible weights and allow the pain in the injured area to determine the rate at which you progress. When you feel a twinge, you've gone too heavy and should reduce the weight by 10 pounds or so.

In all rehabilitation situations, you must be in tune with your body. Sore muscles will tell you when the work load is too great, and twinges of pain in the muscle or joint will let you know when you are going too heavy.

Generally speaking, joints that have been injured will never have the strength they originally possessed, despite corrective surgery, but they will come close. Injured muscles can usually be completely rehabilitated, and the muscles around injured joints can be made much stronger than they were before the injury. Strengthening the muscles surrounding an injured joint can make the joint stronger.

Adhesion pain is common when you've pulled a muscle. The fibers join back together, but some scar tissue is formed. This scar tissue causes individual muscle fibers to adhere to one another. Thus, as a muscle is being worked, these fibers grate against one another, causing pain. Eventually, these adhesions break down, and the pain disappears. Unfortunately, while it lasts, this pain is impossible to distinguish from that which might result from a reinjury, so rehabilitation of torn muscles often takes longer than is actually necessary.

Back Injury

We've studiously avoided mentioning back problems until now because they are such specialized types of injuries. Back strains are fairly typical weight-training injuries, largely because the spine is your body's weakest link.

Human spines were designed to be horizontal, with us in

the quadruped role. Eons ago, when one of our ancestors insisted on standing erect, he doomed millions of people to the misery of backache. A good horizontal structure doesn't necessarily prove to be equally good when moved to a vertical position.

As a result of standing and sitting erect much of the day, the spine gradually compresses. This compression can damage or rupture spinal disks and pinch delicate nerves in the spinal network. And the compression process is speeded up if the spine is made to bear additional weight.

Back problems that are the result of spinal compression can usually be prevented by regularly decompressing or stretching the spine. A simple hanging exercise done daily can give your back the rest it needs. Grasp a high horizontal bar and relax at a dangle below it for a minute or two. Or hang head down from special boots clipped over such a bar. You can hang in this position for five or more minutes, and you can hold weights in your hands for even greater stretch.

Despite hours of stretching, you may experience back pains. The best home remedies are a generous amount of hanging, soaking in hot tubs of water, and back hyperextensions (see Chapter 6) to thoroughly strengthen the supporting muscles along the spine. Try doing two or three sets of 15 to 20 reps three times a week. If the pain persists, consult a chiropractor, osteopath, or physician.

Knee Injury

One common type of joint injury occurs to the knee, and while the cartilage and/or ligament damage is healing, muscle tone, size, and strength are lost. A physical therapist will be the best guide to your work load while rehabilitating a knee, but you can work it daily for several sets of leg extensions and leg curls (see Chapter 5). Let the pain be your guide again, and reduce the work load when you feel a twinge or two.

Leg extensions are usually done isometrically at first, merely holding the leg straight under a load for 10 to 20 seconds. As soon as inner-knee pain diminishes, however, you can begin doing the full range of motion. The same can be done with leg curls, although a joint in a cast tends to lose considerable mobility, which is slow to return. Only constant work to improve the flexibility of a recently injured joint will again give it a full range of motion.

Level One: Beginning Strength Training

5

Level One strength training will get you started on your weight training program. In this chapter you'll begin with a basic group of exercises for free weights, Universal Gyms, and Nautilus machines. You'll use them for the rest of the years you weight train, constantly adding to the group. After this, we'll combine the exercises into several general strength programs, which you can start on immediately. Just choose the routine appropriate to the equipment you have available.

The general programs in this chapter will be of considerable value in improving your sports performance, and you'll begin noticing results almost immediately. If you have had some prior strength training experience, however, you'll want a program that is more specific to your sport. For this purpose, we have developed strength training routines for a number of specific sports. They are in Chapter 8. Regardless of what training program you choose from this book, it will be suitable for both men and women.

Level One is intended for beginners, but the programs can be used by intermediate or advanced trainees. All they need to do is add a few more sets (one or two to each exercise for intermediates and two or three for advanced athletes) in the training routines. And although the programs in this chapter may be fairly elementary to you, be sure to familiarize yourself thoroughly with each exercise. This familiarity will help you avoid injuries and help you start on the programs in Levels Two and Three. These more advanced training programs incorporate many of the exercises presented in this chapter.

BEGINNING STRENGTH TRAINING TECHNIQUES

Exercise Poundages

Because a wide range of individuals—all having varying strength levels—will be using the training routines in this book, it is difficult to recommend a starting poundage for everyone. As a starting point, however, inexperienced male athletes should try one-half of their body weight for all leg and back exercises and one-fourth of their body weight for all other body parts. Lower female levels of the male hormone testosterone will hold most women a little behind men in strength, so they should try two-fifths of body weight for legs and back, and one-fifth for all the other body parts. Neither men nor women should use any weight at first for abdominal exercises.

From the starting points mentioned above, you will need to decide if the weight is too heavy or light and then adjust it accordingly for the next workout. Should you not complete the assigned number of repetitions, or complete them only with great difficulty, the weight is too heavy. And if you breeze through an exercise with no difficulty, the weight is too light.

Athletes with some weight training experience generally have no difficulty deciding what exercise weight is appropriate, because they remember what weight they've used for some exercises and can equate these movements to others. For example, if they've used 80 pounds with a barbell for curls, they'll use 40 pounds in each hand (a total weight of 80 pounds) for dumbbell curls.

The subject of using "maximum weights" for single repetitions will come up again and again in strength training. A maximum single is the absolute highest weight you can use to do one movement of an exercise. This is determined by warming up with lighter weights on a selected movement—for example, the bench press. After two or three sets of 8 to 10 repetitions with a light weight, jump up in 10-pound increments for singles at each weight until you finally fail and your spotter has to rescue you from being pinned under the weight. Your highest successful attempt is your maximum weight for that movement. Of course this poundage will go up as your strength increases, so most athletes will test their strength every four to six weeks. Testing more often than that can lead to overtraining.

Raising Free Weights to Starting Positions

In most instances, you will be able to simply pull or push barbells and dumbbells into the correct starting positions as defined by the exercise photos and the descriptions that follow. The only important point to keep in mind is that your back must be straight and your hips lower than your shoulders when pulling any weight up from the floor. Initiate such pulls with leg strength, and then follow through with your back (i.e., straighten your legs first, and then your back when pulling).

With very heavy weights, you can either take the barbell from a supporting rack, as for squats and bench presses, or have a training partner or two lift it into position for you. Either method is satisfactory, but using a rack will be most utilitarian, because you will occasionally be training with partners who are not available when you need them.

In and Out of Nautilus Machines

The Nautilus exercise directions will tell you to adjust the seat. You can check for correct adjustments as follows: Your shoulder should be slightly below your elbow at the contraction point of the exercise and your elbow should be lined up to rotate along the axis of the cam. If any of the pads roll over your

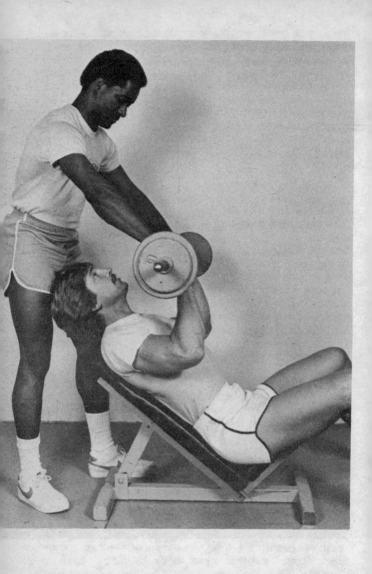

arm or leg as you move it, the seat is not adjusted correctly.

There are two basic groups of Nautilus machines, those with a foot pedal to take resistance off working muscles and those without the pedal feature. If there is a foot pedal on the machine you are using (some arm machines, the pullover machine, chest machine, and some others have this feature), sit in the seat, fasten the lap belt (if there is one), and press down on the pedal enough to slip your arms into the working part of the machine. Let go of the pedal to put full resistance on your arms, and perform the required number of repetitions of the exercise. When finished, press down on the foot pedal to remove the resistance from your arms, slip your arms free, and release the pedal. Unbuckle the seat belt and step free from the machine.

On all non-pedal machines (leg and shoulder machines and some back machines), you need simply to slide your arms or legs away from the moving part and walk away.

LEVEL ONE EXERCISES

The following exercises are the most basic movements for each of the major muscle groups: chest, back, shoulders, arms, abdominals, thighs, and calves. Such basic movements as the bench press, bent row, and squat use groupings of muscles in concert to move the weight. For example, the bench press stimulates the pectorals, deltoids, triceps, and, to a lesser degree, the *latissimus dorsi* and forearm muscles. The bent row works the *latissimus dorsi, trapezius, erector spinae*, biceps, and forearms, while the squat works front thigh, hamstrings, calves, *erector spinae*, and *trapezius*.

For now we'll be doing the most basic movements possible; in later exercises we'll begin to work individual muscles in isolation from the rest of the body. Finally, we'll isolate individual parts of muscle groups from the rest of the muscle. The basic exercises will be presented largely in Level One, the movements isolated to specific muscle groups primarily in Level Two, and the exercises isolated to segments of muscles predominantly in Level Three.

In this and the following two chapters, the exercises presented will be grouped according to what general muscle group they influence most. Within each muscle group category, there will be one or more exercises, depending on how many actual movements are available for that muscle group. Before you perform any exercise, read through all of the instructions, with particular attention to the Biomechanical Tips. They contain safety precautions as well as indications of the physiological benefits of the exercise.

Chest Exercises

BENCH PRESS

Muscles Involved: Primarily the pectorals and deltoids, with triceps as a secondary motivating muscle group. The forearm muscles and *latissimus dorsi* act as stabilizing muscles.

Barbell
Starting Position

Lie back on a flat bench with your head at one end of the bench and your feet flat on the floor at the other end. Take a shoulder

width overhand grip on a barbell handle, palms facing forward perpendicular to the floor. Support the barbell at straight arm's length directly over your chest.

Universal
Starting Position

Lie back on the flat bench at the bench press station with your head at one end of the bench and your feet flat on the floor at the other end. Take a shoulder width overhand grip on the bench press station handles, palms perpendicular to the floor. Straighten your arms so that you are supporting the handles at straight arm's length directly over your chest.

Nautilus
Starting Position

Sit down on the seat of the Nautilus chest machine and lean back on the 45-degree angle back of the seat. Buckle or fasten the seat belt across your lap. Place your feet on the large pedal in front of your legs and grasp the pressing handles with your palms facing each other. With an assisting push from your feet on the pedal, straighten your arms until you are supporting the handles at arm's length straight out from your chest.

Performance

1. Bend your elbows and let the bar or handles descend to chest level.

2. Press back to the starting position by straightening your arms.

3. Repeat as required.

Biomechanical Tips

You will receive maximum pectoral stimulation if your elbows are forced away from your body at right angles to your torso. In this way, the arms are placed in a position where there is direct pull from the pectorals on the attachments to your upper arm bones. This biomechanical position results in a pectoral stimulus superior to that from any other arm position, which builds the best possible quality of chest muscle strength.

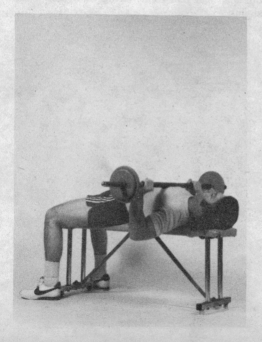

Back Exercises

BENT ROWING

Muscles Involved: Primarily the *latissimus dorsi* of the upper back, with secondary emphasis on biceps, *trapezius, erector spinae,* and forearm muscles.

Barbell
Starting Position

Bend over until your torso is parallel to the floor. Your feet should be about shoulder width apart with toes pointed out slightly. Your arms should be hanging straight down. In this position, grasp a barbell with an overhand grip, your hands one shoulder width apart and your palms facing your shins. Bend your knees slightly.

Performance

1. Pull the barbell up until it touches your lower ribcage.
2. Lower the barbell slowly to the starting point.
3. Repeat.

Biomechanical Tips

Your upper arms should be moved to a 45-degree angle from your torso as the barbell is pulled upward. This results in the most favorable biomechanical position for maximum upper back stimulation. To prevent lower back muscle injuries keep your knees unlocked and tense your spinal muscles enough to bring your spine into a slightly arched position.

LAT MACHINE PULLDOWNS

Muscles Involved: Primarily the *latissimus dorsi*, with secondary emphasis on the biceps, forearms, and posterior deltoids.

Lat Machine or Universal Starting Position

Sit or kneel down under the free-weight lat machine or the lat machine pulldown station on a Universal Gym, facing the weight stack. Grasp the handles at the ends of the lat pulley bar with each hand spread six to twelve inches beyond shoulder width. Your palms should be facing forward, away from your body.

Performance

1. Pull the bar down until it touches the base of your neck behind your head.
2. Return to the starting position, arms straight, and pull the next rep to the front of your neck.
3. Alternate pulling to back and front as required.

Biomechanical Tips

Kinesiologists tell us the function of the *latissimus dorsi* is to pull the upper arms down and back, so emphasize pulling your elbows down and back on each repetition.

NAUTILUS PULLOVERS

Muscles Involved: Primarily the *latissimus dorsi*, with secondary emphasis on the pectorals and abdominals. The *latissimus dorsi* muscle group comes into play quite strongly when pulling objects toward you, as in grasping a wrestling opponent.

Nautilus
Starting Position

Adjust the machine's seat up or down until a line passing through both shoulder points would also pass through the middle of the Nautilus cam (which looks like a schematic of a snail shell). Sit down, buckle the seat belt across your lap, and place your feet on the pedal. Push down on the pedal until you can put your elbows on the large pads attached to the movement arm. The outer part of your upper arm should be resting against the outer angled pad on each side. Grasp the bar behind your head. Let go of the pedal with your feet. Let your elbows travel back as far behind your head as possible.

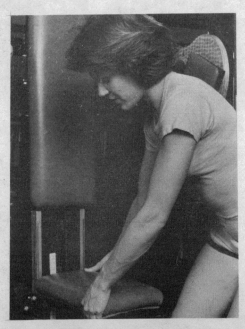

Performance

1. Push the pads in a semicircle with your elbows to a point as far forward and down as you can. Usually this finishing point will be reached when the elbow pads or the bar across the movement arm comes in contact with your sides or lower abdomen.

2. Return along the same arc to the starting position.

3. Repeat as required.

Biomechanical Tips

On the Nautilus pullover machine, little can go wrong if you follow the description and illustrations. If you get stuck anywhere along the arc of the movement and can't finish a rep, just hit the foot pedal, which will release the pressure so you can remove your arms from the machine. On the Nautilus pullover machine, you can put your upper arms through approximately a 200-degree range of motion, more than double what you can achieve with bent rows or lat machine pulldowns.

DEADLIFTS

Muscles Involved: Primarily the *erector spinae* and front thighs, with secondary emphasis on the upper back muscles, forearms, hamstrings, and hip extensors. The abdominals and calves act as stabilizing muscles. Deadlifts are important to strengthen the muscles used to pull anything up from the ground, as in lifting a wrestling opponent from the mat.

Barbell
Starting Position

Stand up to a heavy barbell until your shins rest against the handle. Your feet should be about shoulder width apart and your toes, pointed slightly outward. Bend down and grasp the barbell handle with an overhand grip, your hands about shoulder width apart and your palms facing toward your shins. Bend your legs until your hips are below your shoulders and slightly above your knees. Arch your back slightly by tensing your lower back muscles (*erector spinae*). Keep your head upright throughout the exercise and look straight ahead.

Performance

1. Pull the barbell up along your legs, first by straightening your legs and then extending at the hips to bring your body upright. When your body is completely straight and upright, the barbell will be resting across the tops of your thighs.
2. Lower the barbell slowly back along the same path, flexing at the hips first and then the legs as you return to the starting position.
3. Repeat as required.

Biomechanical Tips

It is vitally important to keep the leg straightening/hip extension sequence as you raise the weight and hip flexion/leg bending sequence as you lower the barbell. When straightening your legs to lift the weight, keep the bar as close to your body as possible. This minimizes the danger of lower back strain. In Chapter 7 we will give you a method of deadlifting during which you can keep your legs straight, but for now be very careful to follow the correct leg straightening/hip extension sequence. If you would like additional *trapezius* strengthening, try shrugging your shoulders up and back at the finish of each deadlift.

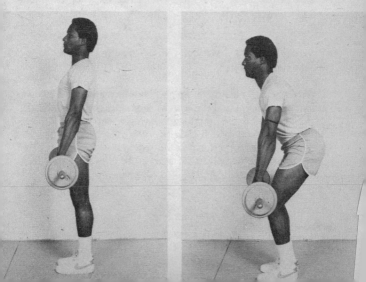

Shoulder Exercises

MILITARY PRESS

Muscles Involved: Primarily the deltoids of your shoulders and the triceps on the back of your upper arms, with secondary emphasis on the upper pectorals and *trapezius*. The lower back, abdominals, and legs act as stabilizers.

Barbell
Starting Position

With feet about shoulder width apart and toes pointed slightly outward, take a shoulder width overhand grip on a barbell as it lies on the floor at your feet. Your palms should be facing your ankles. Stand erect, first straightening your legs and then extending at your hips. Bring the barbell to your shoulders so that it rests at the base of your neck and across your shoulders in front of your neck.

Performance

1. Push the barbell straight up past your face until your elbows are locked straight and the weight is directly over your head.
2. Bend your elbows to return the weight to your shoulders.
3. Repeat.
4. Once you have performed the required number of repetitions, return the barbell to the floor by bending first your legs and then flexing your hips as you lower it.

Biomechanical Tips

Minimize bending backward as you press the bar up. Excessive bending action will make the bar go up easier, but it will also put an unnecessary strain on your lower back. Be sure, as well, that the bar doesn't hit your nose on the way up. That could deviate your septum. Such an injury occurred recently at Gold's Gym.

SEATED PRESS

Muscles Involved: Primarily the deltoids and triceps, with secondary emphasis on the upper chest and *trapezius*. The lower back, abdominals, and legs act as stabilizers.

Barbell
Starting Position

Sit down on one end of a flat bench and plant your feet firmly on the floor to stabilize your body. Grasp a barbell and hold it at the shoulders in exactly the same position as that for a military press. (If you are working with a heavy weight, bring the barbell to your shoulders before sitting down.)

Universal
Starting Position

Sit on the Universal Gym stool directly under the pressing station handles, facing the machine, and grasp the handles with an overhand grip, your palms facing away from your body and about a shoulder width apart.

Nautilus
Starting Position

Adjust the seat up until you can grasp the handles exactly at shoulder height. Your palms should be facing each other and you should be sitting in the seat with your back against the vertical back of the seat. Fasten the seat belt across your lap and cross your ankles directly under your knees.

Performance

1. Push the barbell or handles straight up until your elbows are locked and the barbell or apparatus is directly above your head.

2. Bend your elbows to lower to the starting position.
3. Repeat as required.

Biomechanical Tips

Try to keep your feet off the floor on both the Universal and Nautilus machines, because they will aid in pushing up the weight and you should be isolating the tension of your deltoids and triceps. You will find with a barbell that you can press about 10 to 15 percent less weight for the same number of repetitions while seated than you can when standing and doing military presses. The reason is that sitting isolates your legs from the movement.

DUMBBELL PRESS

Muscles Involved: Primarily the deltoids and triceps, with secondary emphasis on the upper pectoral and *trapezius*. The lower back, abdominals, and legs act as stabilizers. Strong deltoids are needed in all sports.

Dumbbell Starting Position

Stand erect, your feet shoulder width apart and your toes slightly outward, a dumbbell in each hand. Bring the dumbbells to your shoulders as if preparing for a military press with a barbell. At your shoulders, your palms should be facing forward, the same as for a military press.

Performance

1. Push the dumbbells straight up to arm's length overhead, the two inner plates together.

2. Bend your elbows and return the dumbbells to the starting position.

3. Repeat as required.

Biomechanical Tips

The primary advantages of pressing dumbbells in place of a barbell are greater range of motion and the possibility of varied hand positions. With dumbbells you can lower your hands below the level of your shoulders, while a barbell would run into your shoulder muscles before your hands could be lowered to the full possible extent of the pressing range of motion. Besides facing your palms forward when you press dumbbells, you can try facing them toward each other, or at any other angle you desire. For added shoulder and triceps isolation, you can also do dumbbell presses while seated in the same manner you did seated barbell presses.

Upper Arm Exercises

BARBELL CURLS

Muscles Involved: Primarily the biceps and *brachialis*, with secondary emphasis on the forearms. Your biceps muscles are important in any sports activity in which your arms must be bent under resistance, such as when rowing or doing certain gymnastic movements.

Barbell
Starting Position

Stand erect with your feet about shoulder width apart and your toes facing slightly outward. Grasp a barbell with an underhand grip, your hands one shoulder width apart and your palms

facing away from your ankles. Rest the barbell across the tops of your thighs in the same manner as at the finish of a deadlift.

Performance

1. Pin your upper arms to your sides and move the bar in a semicircle from the tops of your thighs to your throat using only the strength of your biceps.
2. Return along the same arc to the starting position.
3. Repeat as required.

Biomechanical Tips

Be careful to keep your upper body rigid and motionless as you do curls. Swinging the torso back and forth removes much of the stress from your biceps. To make this rigid stance easy, stand with your back against a post or the wall.

PULLEY CURLS

Muscles Involved: Primarily the biceps and *brachialis*, with secondary emphasis on the forearm muscles.

Universal
Starting Position

Stand erect with your feet about shoulder width apart and your toes pointed slightly outward about six to twelve inches back from the pulley. Grasp the low pulley handle on a Universal Gym with an underhand grip, your palms facing away from your body about twelve to fifteen inches apart. Rest the handle across your upper thighs in the same position a barbell would be for barbell curls.

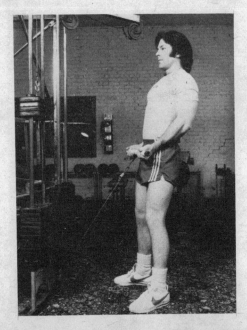

Performance

1. Pin your upper arms to your sides and move the pulley handle in a semicircle from your thighs to your chin.
2. Return to the start.
3. Repeat the movement as required.

Biomechanical Tips

On this and all other curling movements, be careful to keep your elbows against your sides. Letting them drift outward during a curl will take stress off the biceps, the same as swinging your upper body does.

REVERSE
BARBELL CURLS

Muscles Involved: Primarily the *brachialis* and the biceps muscles. The wrist extensors play a secondary role in supporting the wrist position. Reverse curls are the most direct exercise you can do for the *brachialis* muscle, which lies under the biceps on your upper arm.

Barbell
Starting Position

Assume exactly the same starting position as you would for a barbell curl, *except* your palms should be facing toward instead of away from your body. This overhand grip is called a reverse grip.

Performance

1. With your upper arms pinned to your sides, move the barbell in a semicircle from the tops of your thighs to your chin.
2. Return along the same arc to the starting point.
3. Repeat as required.

Biomechanical Tips

Many strength trainees have found a grip in the center of the barbell with index fingers about six inches apart to be superior to a shoulder width grip. Try both in your training programs and decide which you like best.

SEATED
NAUTILUS CURLS

Muscles Involved: Primarily the biceps and *brachialis*, with secondary emphasis on the forearms.

Nautilus
Starting Position

Adjust the seat to a height at which you can sit on it and comfortably drape your arms over the angled padding, hands toward the bottom of the pad and the backs of your upper arms resting on the pads. Fasten the seat belt across your lap and push down on the foot pedal to raise the small pads attached to the movement arm enough to slip your wrists under them. At the start, your wrists will be resting under the pads, your palms up, and your arms perfectly straight. Let go of the foot pedal and put the machine's resistance on your wrists.

Performance

1. Curl your wrist up in a semicircle to the full extent of your range of motion.
2. Return to your starting position.
3. Repeat as required.
4. Use the foot pedal again to remove your wrists from the pads at the completion of your set.

Biomechanical tips

Try curling the weight up more slowly than usual and pausing for a three count at the top of the movement before lowering. You won't be able to use a heavy weight, but this technique will result in a maximum biceps contraction.

LYING BARBELL TRICEPS EXTENSIONS

Muscles Involved: Primarily the triceps on the backs of your upper arms, with secondary emphasis on forearms.

Barbell
Starting Position

Lie back on a flat bench with your head at one end and feet flat on the floor on either side of the bench to balance your body. Take a narrow overhand grip (six inches or less between your hands) on a barbell, being careful to balance your grip in the middle of the bar. Start with the barbell grasped with arms straight over your chest, palms perpendicular to the floor, and facing toward your feet.

Performance

1. Keeping your upper arms absolutely stationary, lower the barbell in a semicircle from the starting point until it touches your forehead.
2. Return along the same arc with triceps strength until you are again back to the starting position.
3. Repeat as required.

Biomechanical Tips

Never allow your elbows to flare out to the sides as you do triceps extensions because this movement will take considerable stress off your triceps.

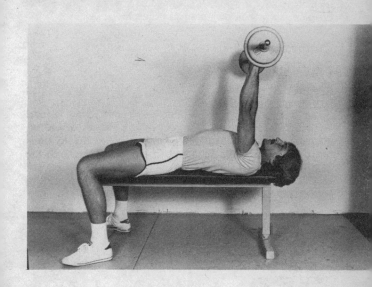

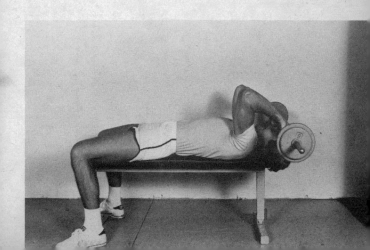

DUMBBELL TRICEPS EXTENSIONS

Muscles Involved: Primarily the triceps, with secondary emphasis on the forearms. Triceps strength is essential in any athletic activity in which you straighten your arm from a bent position, such as throwing a ball or javelin.

Dumbbell Starting Position

Stand with your feet about shoulder width apart. Grasp a single dumbbell in both hands, with your fingers interlaced, and extend your arms with the dumbbell in your hands directly overhead until your elbows are locked. The dumbbell handle should be perpendicular to the floor with your hands touching the under side of the top plate, and the bottom plate hanging down below your hands.

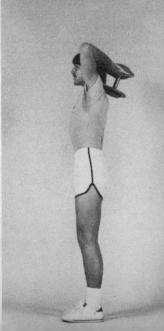

Performance

1. Keep your upper arms stationary and bend at the elbows to let the dumbbell move in a semicircle from the starting point until it touches the back of your neck.
2. Extend your arms back to the start with triceps power, being careful not to move your upper arms.
3. Repeat for the required number of repetitions.

Biomechanical Tips

For variety, you can also do dumbbell triceps extensions with one arm at a time, the dumbbell held in the exercising hand, or you can do the exercise with both hands at a time and two dumbbells, one in each hand.

NAUTILUS TRICEPS EXTENSIONS

Muscles Involved: Primarily the triceps, with minimal emphasis on forearms.

Nautilus Starting Position

Adjust the seat up or down so that the backs of your upper arms rest comfortably on the large lower pad as you sit in the seat. Place your hands against the small pads. Fasten the lap belt and push on the foot pedal to raise the extension apparatus so that your wrists rest against the small pads on the extension arm, palms open and faeing each other. Let go of the foot pedal to place resistance on your wrists and bend your arms as fully as you can.

Performance

1. Straighten your arms with triceps power.
2. Return to the starting position.
3. Repeat as required.
4. Let the weights return over your head before you get off the machine. (When you have finished your set, push on the foot pedal to take the weight off your wrists long enough to remove your arms from the apparatus.)

Biomechanical Tips

Be sure to keep your elbows anchored to the elbow pads throughout the exercise. You can also occasionally try this movement with your palms facing away to attack the triceps from a slightly different angle.

LAT MACHINE PUSHDOWNS

Muscles Involved: Primarily the triceps, with secondary emphasis on the forearm muscles.

Lat Machine or Universal Starting Position

Stand with feet about shoulder width apart and twelve inches behind where the free-weight or Universal Gym lat machine bar hangs down. Take a six-inch-wide overhand grip in the middle of the lat bar, palms facing toward the floor. Pull the bar down to your thighs to a position where your elbows are locked.

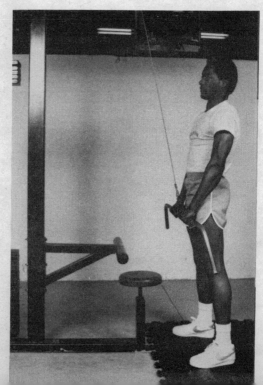

Performance

1. Pin your elbows to your sides and slowly bend your arms to full flexion, allowing the bar to travel in a semicircle from your thighs to your chin.
2. Extend your arms with triceps power until they are again straight.
3. Repeat the movement as required.

Biomechanical Tips

Lean slightly in toward the bar to put your triceps into the most favorable mechanical position for pushing the bar back down to your thighs each rep. You will also find the movement a little more comfortable if you keep your wrists cocked (bent forward) throughout the movement.

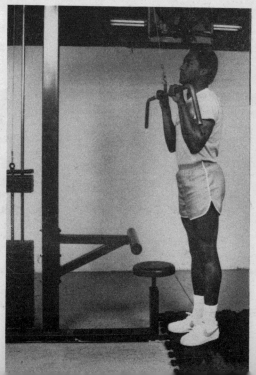

Abdominal Exercises

LEG RAISES

Muscles Involved: The frontal abdominals and the hip flexors (*psoas* and *iliacus*).

Free-Weight
or Universal
Starting Position

Lie down on your back on a sit-up board, either a free-weight version or the one on a Universal Gym, and grasp the foot straps or rollers with your hands. Bend your knees at a 30-degree angle.

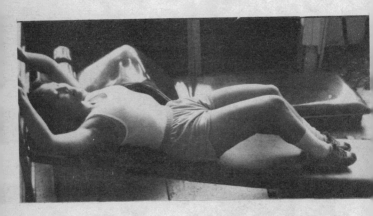

Performance

1. Raise your legs straight up until your knees come within about six inches of your face, keeping the knees bent at a 30-degree angle. Your feet will travel along an approximate 180-degree arc during the movement.
2. Lower your legs.
3. Repeat as required.

Biomechanical Tips

By keeping your knees bent, you reduce potentially harmful strain on your lower back.

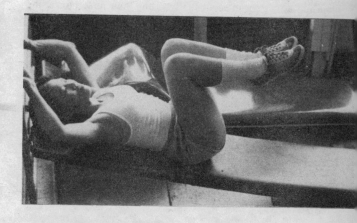

SIT-UPS

Muscles Involved: The frontal abdominals and the hip flexors (*psoas* and *iliacus*).

Free-Weight or Universal Starting Position

Lie down on your back on an abdominal board, either a free-incline or the bench on a Universal Gym, and hook your feet under the foot straps or rollers. Bend your knees at a 30-degree angle and interlace your fingers behind your head.

Performance

1. *Curl* your torso up until your elbows touch your knees. By curling up we mean sequentially lifting your torso up starting with your upper back, then the middle of your back, and finally your lower back.
2. Return in the opposite sequence (lower back, middle back, upper back) to the starting point.
3. Repeat as required.

Biomechanical Tips

Bending your legs eases strain on your lower back when doing sit-ups. When you are performing sit-ups correctly, your movement will be slow and controlled. Jerking your torso upright, like many ill-informed strength trainees do, is a total waste of the movement.

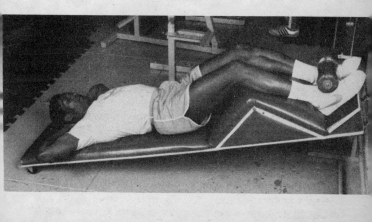

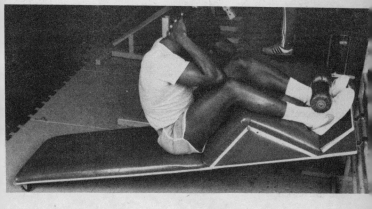

NAUTILUS KNEE PULL-UPS

Muscles Involved: The frontal abdominals and the hip flexors (*psoas* and *iliacus*).

Nautilus Starting Position

Sit on the edge of the bench facing the movable roller pad. Fasten the seat belt around your waist, and then pull up the roller with your arms and slide your knees under the pad. Lie back, allowing your legs to descend with the rollers, and grasp the handles by the sides of your hips to steady your body. Cross your ankles.

Performance

1. Raise your knees up to a point as close to your chest as possible.
2. Lower as far as you can.
3. Repeat the movement as required.

Biomechanical Tips

If this machine ever gives you any pain in your lower back or you notice a clicking sensation in the same area, immediately abandon using it and substitute sit-ups instead. A few individuals have weak lower back structures, and they can be injured by doing this movement.

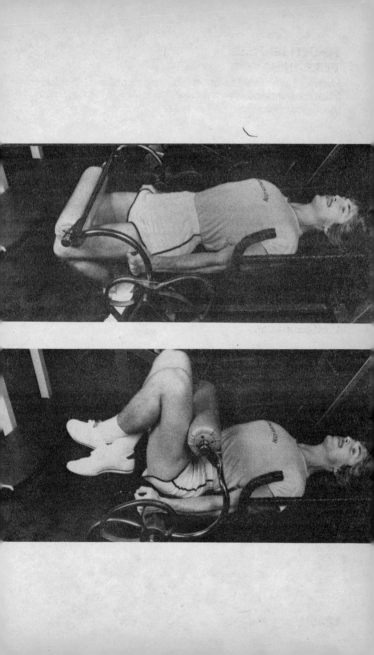

KNEE-UPS

Muscles Involved: The frontal abdominals and the hip flexors (*psoas* and *iliacus*).

Free-Apparatus Starting Position

Sit on one end of a flat bench with your legs extending away from the end of the bench. Lean your torso back at about a 45-degree angle from vertical and grasp the sides of the bench with your arms to steady your upper body. At this point your arms will be either straight or slightly bent, depending on how long your torso is in relation to your arms. Extend your legs out and down at an approximate 45-degree angle from horizontal, your feet and legs held together, knees straight, and your heels one or two inches from the floor. If you like, you can point your toes.

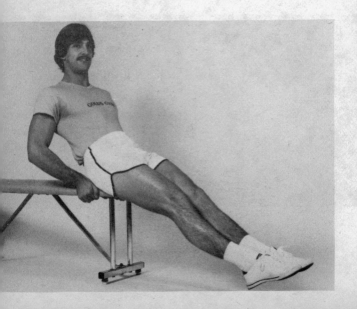

Performance

1. Maintaining the same upper body position throughout the movement, slowly bend your knees and raise them up to your chest. When your knees touch your chest, your legs should be fully bent.
2. Lower along the same arc to the starting position.
3. Repeat as required.

Biomechanical Tips

This movement is very similar to the Nautilus Knee Pull-Ups, so if you feel pains or clicks in your lumbar region, you should also discontinue doing knee-ups to avoid a lower back injury. Knee-ups are a rather low-intensity abdominal movement, so athletes who have difficulty doing sit-ups or leg raises can rely on knee-ups to build the strength necessary to do the more difficult abdominal exercises. In general, strong abdominals and hip flexors are required in any sports activity in which you bring your torso and legs toward each other, such as diving or tumbling in gymnastics.

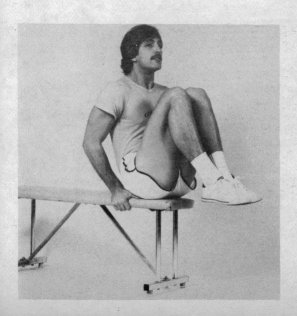

Thigh Exercises

SQUATS

Muscles Involved: Primarily the front thighs and gluteal muscles of the buttocks, with secondary emphasis on the hamstrings, lower back, and the supporting muscles of the abdomen.

Barbell
Starting Position

Stand with your feet parallel about shoulder width apart, the toes pointed outward at a 35- to 45-degree angle from a foot parallel position. Place a barbell across your shoulders and behind your neck, centering it and balancing it in place by grasping the bar with your hands out near the plates, palms facing forward. Keep your body upright throughout the movement.

Performance

1. Bend your knees and sink down in a deep knee-bend until your thighs are parallel to the floor.
2. Return to the upright position.
3. Repeat as required.
Note: With light weights you will be able to place the bar behind your neck with arm strength, but as you progress it will be best to load up the barbell on a squat rack and take it off the rack for each set.

Biomechanical Tips

Never bounce at the bottom of any squatting movement, because this puts exceptional strain on knee ligaments and the lower back. Never bend over at the waist during any part of the movement, because this can injure your lower back. To keep your torso upright, pick a focus point for your eyes and keep looking at it as you squat down and come back up. This will keep your head up, which will, in turn, keep your torso upright. If you have difficulty keeping your feet flat on the floor, rest your heels on a 2 × 4-inch board.

PARTIAL SQUATS

Muscles Involved: Primarily the quadriceps of the frontal thigh and gluteal muscles of the buttocks, with secondary emphasis on the hamstrings, lower back, and supporting muscles of the abdominals.

Barbell
Starting Position

Because you will be doing less-than-full repetitions of the squat, the starting position for partial squats is the same as for full squats.

Performance

There are four common types of partial squats—quarter squats (one-fourth of the way down), half squats, three-quarter squats, and bench squats. Bench squats are done to a depth at which your buttocks touch a bench that you are straddling while doing the movement. Other than the depth, partial squats are performed exactly like full squats.

Biomechanical Tips

Because you will be able to use significantly more weight for partial squats than for full squats, it will be a good idea to concentrate on keeping your back muscles under tension throughout the movement. This will prevent you from relaxing at any point in the movement, which can leave your lower back vulnerable to injury. Keeping the back muscles tensed is vital when doing bench squats, because there is a natural tendency to sit on the bench for a moment at the bottom of each repetition. To prevent this, try to just "touch" the bench before starting up. Never, however, bounce on the bench when doing bench squats. For all squatting movements, you can also use a weight-lifting belt (more on this later) to give added support to your abdomen and lumbar muscles.

LEG PRESS

Muscles Involved: Primarily the quadriceps of the frontal thigh and gluteals of the buttocks, with secondary emphasis on the hamstrings. Your arms and upper back will provide a supporting action.

Universal
Starting Position

Sit in the leg press station seat, grasp the handles on both sides of your seat, and place your feet on the lower set of pedals, your insteps centered on the pedals.

Nautilus
Starting Position

Sit in the Nautilus leg press machine seat and fasten the lap belt. Place your feet flat on the pedals in front of you, centering the feet on the pads. Your legs will be bent at a 90-degree angle when the seat is adjusted far enough forward. Grasp the handles at the sides of your hips.

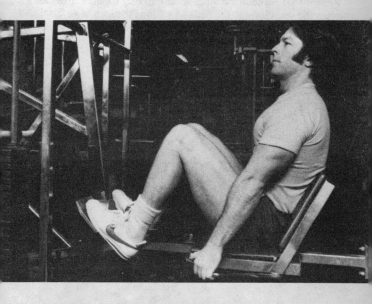

Performance

1. Push your legs straight out with thigh strength until your knees lock.
2. Return to the starting position.
3. Repeat as required.

Biomechanical Tips

If you use the top set of pedals (provided your machine has two sets—some don't), the weight will be 50 percent greater than on the bottom set of pedals, and you will work the gluteals more strongly; however, the range of motion will be decreased by about 20 percent. For increased range of motion, you can move the seat closer to the pedals by lifting the inch-wide black knob at the front of the seat. With the knob lifted, slide the seat forward to the point you desire, release the knob, and let the seat lock into place.

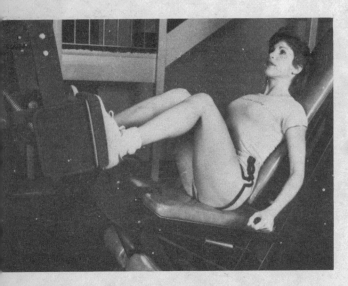

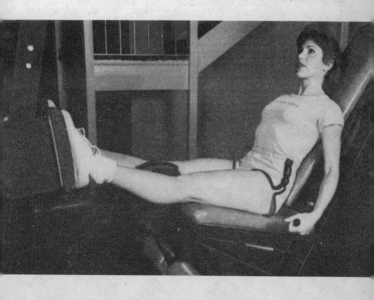

LEG EXTENSIONS

Muscles Involved: Almost totally the quadriceps, with a minimum of support from the arms, abdominals, and both upper and lower back. Quadriceps strength is helpful in any movement during which you extend your legs from a partially or fully bent position, such as when running or jumping.

Free-Weight Starting Position

Sit on the edge of a free-weight leg-extension machine and hook the tops of your feet under the lower set of rollers. Steady your upper body by grasping the sides of the bench beside your hips.

Universal Starting Position

This starting position is exactly the same as on the free-weight leg-extension machine. (Not shown.)

Nautilus Starting Position

Adjust the back of the bench forward by lifting the handle on the right side of the machine as you are sitting in it (some machines will not be adjustable) until you can sit and lean back while the backs of your knees extend no more than one inch past the front edge of the bench. There will be only one set of rollers on a Nautilus leg-extension machine, so place the tops of your feet under them. Fasten the lap belt, and grasp the handles at the sides of your hips to steady your upper body.

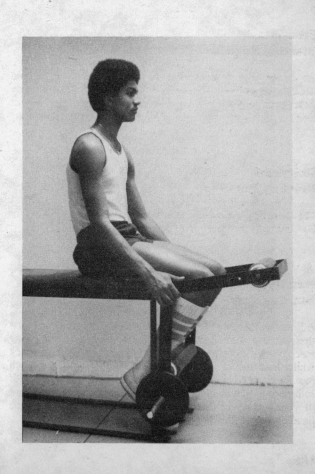

Performance

1. Fully extend your legs with quadriceps strength until your knees lock.
2. Pause in the top position for one count.
3. Lower to the starting position.
4. Repeat as required.

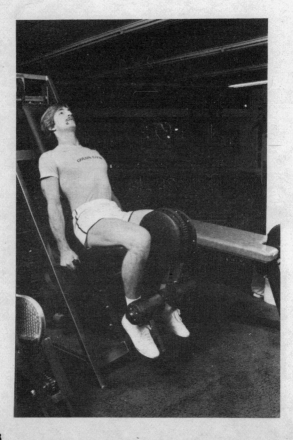

Biomechanical Tips

Alternate foot position occasionally, doing some sets with your feet parallel, some with toes pointed out at a 45-degree angle, and others with the toes pointed in at 45-degrees. Using all three toe positions will build more complete strength in the quadriceps.

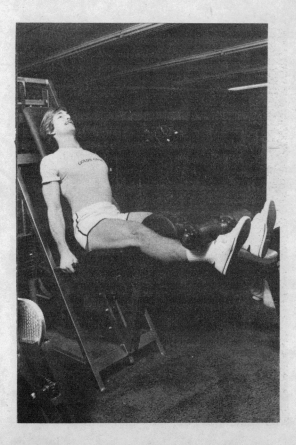

LEG CURLS

Muscles Involved: Primarily the hamstrings, with secondary emphasis on the calves and buttocks. Hamstring strength is helpful in all athletic movements in which you bend your legs from a straight position such as sprinting and jumping.

Free-Weight
Starting Position

Lie face down or chest down on a free-weight leg curl table with your knees extending one or two inches over the edge of the table. Hook your heels under the upper set of rollers and grasp the edge of the bench in front of your head to steady your body. Straighten your knees.

Universal
Starting Position

This starting position is exactly the same as on the free-weight leg curl machine. (Not shown.)

Nautilus
Starting Position

There will be only one set of rollers on a Nautilus leg curl machine, so lie down as on the free-weight machine and hook your heels under the rollers. Grasp the handles at the sides of the bench to steady your body. Straighten your knees.

Performance

1. Bend your legs at the knees as much as possible using hamstring strength.
2. Lower to the starting position.
3. Repeat as required.

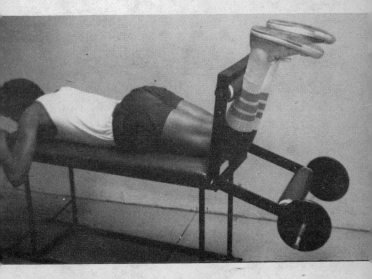

Biomechanical Tips

Again, use all three foot positions recommended for the leg extensions. It is also important not to lift your hips up from the bench as you do leg curls, because this procedure shortens the range of motion.

Calf Exercises

BARBELL RISE
ON TOES

Muscles Involved: Primarily the calves, with slight supporting assistance from the thighs, back, and abdominals.

Barbell
Starting Position

Put a barbell behind your neck in exactly the same manner as for the start of a squat. Put the balls of your feet on a four-inch-thick wooden block and stretch your heels down as far as is comfortable below your toes.

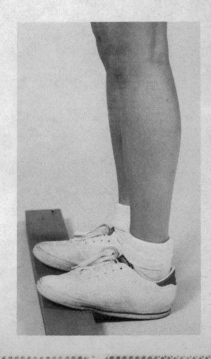

Performance

1. Rise up as high as you can on your toes.
2. Return to the starting position.
3. Repeat as required.

Biomechanical Tips

This exercise will usually be difficult to do without losing your balance. Only by doing the movement slowly is it possible to retain your balance. The balance factor is what eventually led to the invention of calf machines.

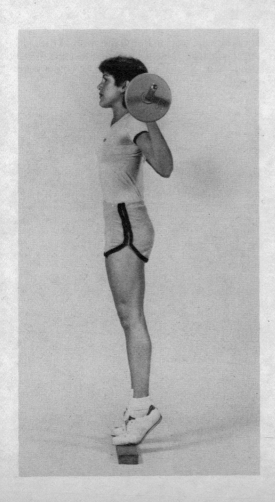

CALF MACHINE

Muscles Involved: Primarily the calves, with slight supporting assistance from the thighs, back, and abdominals.

Calf Machine
Starting Position

Stand erect, facing into the machine, with the yokes of the calf machine on your shoulders and the balls of your feet on a four-inch-thick wooden block. Stretch your heels as far below your toes as is comfortable.

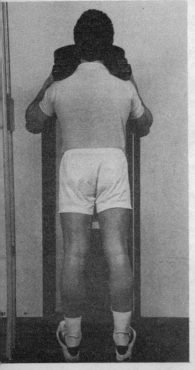
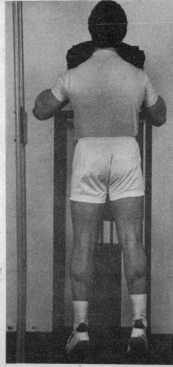

Performance

1. Rise on your toes as high as you can.
2. Return to starting position.
3. Repeat as required.
Note: The block on all calf exercises allows you to stretch your heels down for a much longer range of motion than would be possible standing flat on the floor.

Biomechanical Tips

For more complete calf strength development, alternate between each of the three toe positions mentioned for use with leg extensions and leg curls: toes in, straight, and out. Use the foot placement variations on all calf exercises.

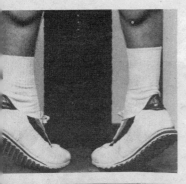

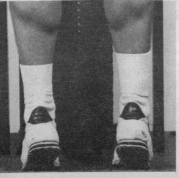

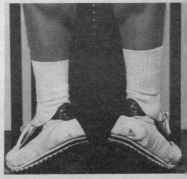

CALF PRESS

Muscles Involved: Primarily the calves, with slight support from the thighs, arms, back, and abdominals. Calf strength is important in all athletic movements during which you extend your toes, such as when sprinting and jumping.

Universal
Starting Position

Sit in the seat and assume the legs-straight position of a leg press. Slide your feet off the pedals until only the balls of your feet are in contact with the apparatus. Flex your toes toward your knees as far as possible.

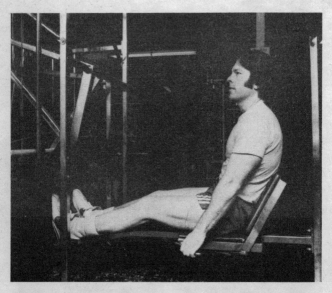

Nautilus
Starting Position

Sit in the apparatus and assume the legs-straight position of a leg press. Slide your feet off the pedals until only the balls of your feet are in contact with the apparatus. Flex your toes toward your knees as far as possible.

Performance

1. Extend your toes as far as possible.
2. Return to the starting position:
3. Repeat as required.

Biomechanical Tips

On this and all calf exercises, you should be using all three toe positions. Be sure to keep your legs straight at all times, or your thighs will help to push and the calves will lose part of the resistance. This movement is best when restricted as much as possible to the calf muscles alone.

BASIC ROUTINES: GENERAL STRENGTH-TRAINING PROGRAMS

The following sets of programs are for free weights, Universal, and Nautilus. There will be six basic routines, one for each mode and three more with various combinations of these three training modes. The exercises in each of these training routines are taken from the preceding basic group of exercises. Each program strengthens the body's major muscle groups. Simply select the workout you can do most easily with the equipment available to you.

Free-Weight Program

Exercise	Sets	Rep Range
Squats	3	10–15
Leg Curls	2	10–15
Calf Machine	3	20–30
Bent Rowing	3	8–10
Bench Press	3	6–8
Military Press	2	6–8
Lying Triceps Extensions	2	10–15
Barbell Curls	3	8–10
Leg Raises	1	50+

Universal Gym Program

Exercise	Sets	Rep Range
Leg Press	3	10–15
Leg Curls	2	10–15
Calf Press	3	20–30
Lat Machine Pulldowns	3	8–10
Bench Press	3	6–8
Seated Press	2	6–8
Lat Machine Pushdowns	2	10–15
Pulley Curls	3	8–10
Sit-Ups	1	50+

Nautilus Program

Exercise	Sets	Rep Range
Leg Extensions	2	10–15
Leg Curls	1	10–15
Calf Press	2	20–30
Pullovers	2	8–10
Bench Press	2	6–8
Seated Press	1	6–8
Triceps Extensions	1	10–15
Curls	2	8–10
Knee Pull-Ups	1	15–20

Note: As you may recall from the discussion of Nautilus in Chapter 3, the machines are designed to give very intense exercise. For this reason fewer sets should be done for the Nautilus program.

Barbell/Nautilus
Combined Program

Exercise	Sets	Rep Range
Bench Squats	3	10–15
Nautilus Leg Curls	1	10–15
Calf Machine	3	20–30
Nautilus Pullovers	2	8–10
Nautilus Seated Press	1	6–8
Dumbbell Triceps Extensions	2	10–15
Barbell Curls	3	8–10
Sit-Ups	1	50+

Barbell/Universal Gym
Combined Program

Exercise	Sets	Rep Range
Leg Press	3	10–15
Leg Curls	2	10–15
Calf Machine	3	20–30
Deadlifts	1	10–15
Lat Machine Pulldowns	3	8–10
Barbell Bench Press	3	6–8
Seated Press	2	6–8
Barbell Curls	3	8–10
Leg Raises	1	50+

Barbell/Universal/ Nautilus Combined Program

Exercise	Sets	Rep Range
Leg Press	3	10–15
Nautilus Leg Curls	2	10–15
Calf Machine	3	20–30
Nautilus Pullovers	2	8–10
Barbell Bench Press	3	6–8
Dumbbell Press	2	6–8
Lat Machine Pushdowns	2	10–15
Barbell Curls	3	8–10
Sit-Ups	1	50+

Level Two: Intermediate Strength Training

6

The beginner's training programs in Chapter 5 laid the groundwork for the intermediate work in this chapter. The intermediate level is for athletes who have done Level One strength workouts for two to six months, and the exercises are a little more isolated in nature for Level Two than they were for Level One. Some individuals might be ready for the intermediate level six to eight weeks after starting weight workouts, while a few others may need more than six months. Judge your progress toward Level Two by whether or not you can consistently do five or more sets per body part on the Level One programs. If you can, you're ready for Level Two.

Learning a few intermediate training techniques before you attempt the new exercises and training routines will make your program more individually effective. These techniques include how to gain strength without gaining body weight, how to use a split routine to train more than three times a week, how to use differing repetition schemes to your advantage, how to gain or lose weight, and how long to stay on the programs in the Level One and Level Two chapters.

INTERMEDIATE STRENGTH
TRAINING TECHNIQUES

Strength Gain Without Body Weight Gain

For athletes in various body weight economy sports (e.g., gymnastics, distance running, wrestling, and other weight-class activities), it becomes essential to gain athletic strength without increasing body weight. This is relatively simple if you go about it correctly.

The key to gaining strength while holding down your body weight is to do low numbers of repetitions on all of your sets (reps in the one to three range), while using exercise weights in the range of 80 to 90 percent of your maximum ability for a single repetition in each lift.

To use this system, first calculate your maximum single for one basic exercise per body part (e.g., bench presses for chest, squats for thighs, Nautilus pullovers for back, etc.) using the procedure outlined for this in Chapter 3. Then calculate which weights will be 40, 60, 75, and 90 percent of this figure.

Start the exercise routine by warming up thoroughly with calisthenics and stretching exercises (see Chapter 3). Because you will be using relatively heavy weights when trying to gain strength without a body weight gain, the risk of injury will be greater, and a thorough warm-up is extremely important. Do the calisthenics and stretching and then finish off with some lighter sets of each exercise before doing the heavy work. Here are the approximate weight warm-up sets you should do before doing the strength workout:

1×3 (one set of three reps) at 40 percent of your maximum single
1×3 at 60 percent
1×2 at 75 percent

Follow this warm-up with a strength workout of three sets of one rep at 90 percent of your maximum. The following

156

workout, do four sets of one rep, and the next five sets of one. Once you can do five singles at 90 percent of your maximum, add 5 to 10 pounds of resistance on all sets that you do for that exercise, including the warm-ups, and drop back to three sets of singles on the strength workout portion of the exercise at what will be a new 90 percent figure. By working the sets and weight up in this manner, you will gain strength quickly with minimum body weight increase.

The type of training routine you should follow with the preceding guidelines would be as follows:

Squats: as indicated
Bent Rowing: as indicated
Hyperextensions: 3 sets of 10 to 15 reps with a moderate weight
Lat Machine Pulldowns: 3 sets of 8 reps with 60–70–80 percent of maximum
Incline Press: as indicated
Leg Curls: 3 sets of 10 to 15 sets with 60 percent
Calf Machine: as indicated
Barbell Curls: 3 sets of 8 to 10 reps with 60 percent
Sit-Ups: 1 set of 50 to 100 reps

When using heavy weights, pay strict attention to the biomechanical tips we have been stressing. They will give you correct body positions and minimize the chance of an injury. Use spotters as well, and if you can buy a weight-lifting belt at a sporting goods store, use it on squats, curls, and bent rows.

Weight-lifting belts give support to your back and abdomen. They cost about $25.00 and are of heavy leather, four to six or seven inches wide at the back part of the belt. Try to buy one that's fitted to your waist measurement. If available, we recommend the six-inch-wide belt for athletes over 5′8″ and the four-inch-wide belt for those under this height. Use the belt on all movements in which your back is not supported by weight apparatus and be sure to cinch it down tight.

A final useful injury prevention device is one of those neoprene rubber waistbands many people use to lose fat around their middles. The rubber band does nothing for fat losses, but it is perfect for keeping the lower back and abdomen warm and injury resistant. Such rubber bands are also available for the knees and elbows, two more joints subject to injury, so you might buy them as well. In a sporting goods store, the complete set for waist/back, knees, and elbows will cost you about $20.00 to $25.00.

Split Routines

As long as you are sure to rest each muscle group for at least one full day between exercise days for it, you can begin to train four days a week if you like and later, five or six days. To accomplish this, it is necessary to split the body into halves or thirds. Then work one-half or one-third one day, the next half or third the second day, and the final third or the first half again the third day. Here are three commonly used types of half/half split routines:

First Alternative
Day 1—Upper Body (chest, shoulders, arms, upper back)
Day 2—Lower Body (calves, thighs, lower back, abdominals)
Second Alternative
Day 1—Pushing Muscles (chest, shoulders, triceps, abdominals)
Day 2—Pulling Muscles (back, biceps, thighs, calves)
Third Alternative
Day 1—Torso (chest, shoulders, upper back, abdominals)
Day 2—Arms/Legs (arms, thighs, calves, lower back)

You can do the above alternatives with Day 1 on Mondays and Thursdays and Day 2 on Tuesdays and Fridays, or any other combination similar to this (e.g., Tuesday/Friday and Wednesday/Saturday, or Sunday/Wednesday and Monday/Thursday). Or, you can make the exercise days a little more frequent by following a three-day cycle of Day 1/Day 2/Rest Day. This gives you a fraction more of a workout day each week than does the four-day program, but such a sequence occasionally ruins a weekend that could have been spent in some nonathletic recreational activity.

To go to five days a week, try training Monday through Friday on a Day 1–2–1–2–1 sequence, resting on the weekend. The next week your sequence will be 2–1–2–1–2. And finally, for a six-day schedule, simply alternate Day 1 and Day 2

Monday through Saturday, resting on Sunday.

Generally speaking, you'll want to work out only two or three days per week when you are nearing or actually in your sport's season, because at that point you will be seeking only to maintain your strength levels, not increase them. Trying to increase would divert too much energy from your sports performance to your strength training, a self-defeating procedure.

In the off-season (e.g., late fall and winter for a baseball or softball player), go ahead and use the four-, five-, or six-day split routines. They will allow you to work each muscle group more intensely than if you did the whole body in a single session, simply because you will be fresher from doing less weight work each day.

Varying Sets and Reps

By varying the number of sets and reps you do, you can inject additional variety into your athletic strength workouts. While most beginners are on two or three sets of an exercise in the 8 to 12 rep range with a steady poundage, this is only one of several set-and-rep schemes you can use. The first alternative method of combining sets and reps is to go down in reps and up in the resistance used with each set. So instead of doing curls for three sets of 10 reps with 80 pounds, you can use 70 pounds for 12, 80 for 10, and 90 for 8. Besides adding variety to your workouts, this set/rep scheme also builds strength faster than using a steady poundage will.

The second method is similar to the first, except that you use the same number of reps for each set as the poundages go up. This method is usually used in strength workouts with medium reps (in the 4 to 6 rep range), and then the first few sets will be warm-ups. As an example of this technique, you would squat for 5 reps each set while working up in 20-pound increments each set from about 30 to 35 percent of your maximum to the heaviest weight you can manage for the 5 reps.

A third scheme is to lower the weight and increase the reps—or sometimes leave the reps the same—with each set. An example of this would be 90 pounds for 8 reps, 80 for 10, and 70 for 12. This method is a little dangerous if you start with very heavy weights because of the high injury factor, but it does give you more variety to play with if you are at Level Two or Level Three.

The final set/rep scheme for the intermediate stage involves grouping sets and reps in a training routine and then finishing off with a high-rep set with a light weight to completely exhaust the muscle(s) being exercised. Here's an example for the bench press:

1 set of 10 reps for a warm-up
2 sets of 5 reps with a moderate weight
3 sets of 5 reps with a heavy weight
1 set of 15 to 20 reps with a light weight

This final pump set can be used with any kind of movement or workout, and it will yield good results with all, but it seems to be most effective with basic (large muscle group) exercises like squats, bench presses, and bent rows. A pump set is one of the best methods of thoroughly exhausting a muscle group, because with a light weight you can force out far more repetitions and come much closer to exhaustion.

Weight Gain

Some athletes will want to gain weight, especially football players and those track and field athletes in the weight events. Even many athletes in lighter events such as basketball and swimming come into Gold's Gym wanting to add a few pounds of functional muscle. Gaining such solid muscle weight involves a high-protein, increased-calorie diet (several books on nutrition are listed in the bibliography) and a heavy training program.

To formulate any good weight-gaining workout, it is wise to concentrate primarily on the large muscle groups of the body—legs, back, and chest—with low repetitions and heavy weights. This is because there is much more potential for weight gain in big muscle groups than in small ones. Following is a tried and proven weight gaining routine that we often use with athletes at Gold's Gym. In this sample workout, note that the number of repetitions for each set is suggested. Try to add weight to each succeeding set, except for the final light pump set of 15 reps on squats and bench presses. Do all the exercises in strict form, and rest no more than 60 to 90 seconds between sets.

You might also notice that in the sample program the large muscles are put first in the workout. This is so you hit them hardest when you are still fresh from a day of rest. Later in the workout, when you are a little fatigued, you work the smaller muscle groups, which are less important and require less energy.

Monday/Wednesday/Friday

Exercise	Sets	Rep Range
Squats	5	12/8/5/5/15
Nautilus Pullovers	5	15/12/10/8/6
Bench Press	5	10/8/6/4/15
Bent Rowing	4	8/8/8/8
Military Press	3	6/6/6
Barbell Curls	3	10/8/6
Calf Machine	3	20/20/20
Incline Situps	1	25–50

To gain weight, you'll need to develop a caloric surplus each day in your diet/energy expenditure balance, that is, you'll need to take in more calories than you can burn up. To determine approximately how many calories it takes to maintain your present weight, add up the calories you consume for one week and divide by seven for an average daily intake (taking a week and dividing is far more accurate than randomly choosing a single day, during which your food intake may be far from typical).

Add about 10 percent more calories to your diet than what you're now eating, but be careful to choose this surplus from high protein foods such as meat, poultry, fish, eggs, and milk products. Also be careful to take a multivitamin/mineral capsule with each meal as insurance against dietary deficiencies, some of which can retard weight gains.

Once you have added the surplus calories to your diet, it's essential to keep your daily caloric expenditure at the same level it was when you calculated the maintenance calorie level. To keep from expending calories unnecessarily to maintain that

161

excess, take a half hour nap each day, sleep a full eight hours at night, and avoid excessive aerobic activities, such as long runs or bicycle rides, which are endurance activities that require oxygen for energy release.

By combining diet, exercise, and life-style to create a caloric surplus, you can expect to gain as much as three to five pounds a month for the first two or three months on the program, and about a pound a month after that. Putting on more than this amount will probably result in too much fat accumulation, which will retard rather than aid your athletic progress.

Weight Loss

To lose weight, it is necessary to reverse the procedure for gaining weight and to create a caloric deficit. This is done by cutting food intake calories and/or increasing the number of calories expended each day through exercise. To cut your food intake calories calculate the number of calories needed to maintain your present body weight and reduce that number by 5 to 10 percent each day (see the books listed in Suggested Reading if you want a tested weight reduction diet). To increase caloric expenditure, you can add more physical activity each day. Do an occasional two- or three-mile run, or bike to workouts and back. Swim occasionally and take long walks.

Burning calories with weight training is best done by doing many sets of high repetitions (15 to 50 repetitions) with reduced rest intervals (in the 30 to 60 second range between sets). Here is a sample fat burning strength program:

Monday/Wednesday/Friday

Exercise	Set	Rep Range
Leg Press	3–5	15–20
Leg Curls	3	15–20
Calf Press	3	30–50
Lat Machine Pulldowns	3	15–20
Bench Press	4	10–15
Seated Press	3	10–15
Barbell Curls	4	10–15
Lat Machine Pushdowns	3	15–20
Sit-Ups	3	100+

By going quickly, you should build up a considerable sweat. The amount of perspiration is a good indication of the number of calories you're burning because expended calories raises the body's temperature, and sweating is Nature's way of cooling the body. Just be sure to replace the minerals you sweat out by taking a vitamin/mineral tablet or drinking one of the electrolyte replacement drinks (like ERG or Gatorade) found in most sporting goods stores.

FROM BASIC TO INTERMEDIATE TO ADVANCED: HOW LONG?

Taking into consideration varying rates of progress, you can probably dispense with the basic programs in the preceding chapter after two or three months. And after three to six additional months, the intermediate routines in this chapter will begin to have less relevance. By that time, however, you will have accumulated a fairly good knowledge of strength training from this book, and can easily progress into advanced levels of weight training with a minimum of coaching and the tips in this and the following chapter.

LEVEL TWO EXERCISES

You can now add a number of new exercises to the basic pool. Note that there will be very few Universal Gym movements in this section, because the variety of exercises you can do on that apparatus is limited, and we have already introduced you to most of the Universal Gym exercises at Level One. There will also be fewer Nautilus movements, because you are also approaching the limits of the Nautilus system's versatility.

The exercises in this intermediate section will still include some basic movements that use more than one muscle group to move the weight, but there will be a number of isolation exercises that limit the strength training effect to a single muscle

163

group. And in the next chapter, we will refine this isolation concept even more by presenting exercises that stress only one part of a muscle group. So the three-chapter progress will be from predominantly general exercises to specific movements to even more specific exercises.

Chest Exercises

INCLINE PRESS

Muscles Involved: Primarily the upper pectorals, deltoids, and triceps, with secondary emphasis on the lower pectorals.

Barbell
Starting Position

Lie back on a 45-degree incline bench with your feet flat on the pedals or floor and take a shoulder-width overhand grip on a barbell, palms facing your body as the barbell lies across your thighs. Bring the weight to the base of your neck so that your elbows are directly below the barbell handle.

Universal
Starting Position

Lie back on a 45-degree incline bench under the seated press station of a Universal Gym. Center the bench so your shoulder joints are directly beneath the pressing handles. Move your elbows to a point directly under the handles. Grasp the handles, palms facing up.

Performance

1. Push the weight straight up from the chest until your elbows lock.
2. Lower to the starting point.
3. Repeat as required.

Biomechanical Tips

The elbows must be kept directly under the weight at all times, because this position puts maximum stress on the pectorals and deltoids. While flat bench presses were once the favorite chest exercise of football players, inclines are now most popular, because they more closely simulate the angle at which the arms are extended in driving into an opponent.

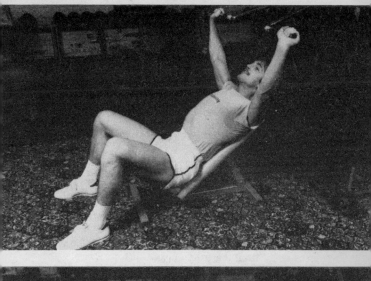

DECLINE PRESS

Muscles Involved: Primarily the lower pectorals and triceps, with secondary emphasis on deltoids and *latissimus dorsi*. Decline presses are intended to isolate the lower pectoral from the rest of the muscle. With the three variations of the bench press we have explored—on a flat, incline, or decline bench—we can now work the whole pectoral at once, or isolate the action to the upper or lower halves of the muscle.

Barbell
Starting Position

Lie back on a 30-degree decline bench, your head at the lower end and your knees hooked over the top of the bench. Take a shoulder-width overhand grip on a barbell, palms facing your feet, and support the barbell at straight arm's length above your chest. Because of the declined position, your arms will be about 60 degrees away from the front of your torso, instead of the 90-degree position they would assume in a flat bench press.

Universal
Starting Position

Lie back on a 30-degree decline bench, your head at the lower end and your knees hooked over the top of the bench. The bench should be positioned so that your shoulder joints are directly under the handles of the Universal Gym bench press station. Grasp the handle with an overhand grip, hands about shoulder width apart, palms facing your feet, and push the handles up until your elbows lock.

Performance

1. Bend your elbows until the barbell or bench press station handles touch your chest at the bottom edge of your pectorals.
2. Press back to the starting position.
3. Repeat as required.

Biomechanical Tips

To put your pectorals in the best position to develop strength, keep your elbows directly under the barbell or pressing handles throughout the movement.

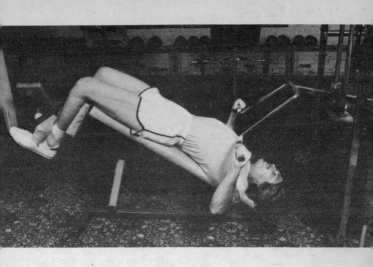

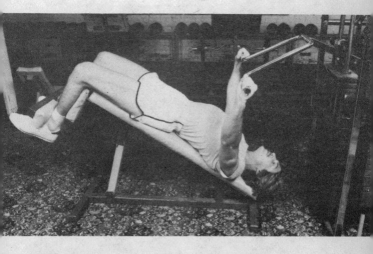

173

PARALLEL BAR DIPS

Muscles Involved: Primarily the lower pectorals, deltoids, and triceps, with secondary emphasis on upper pectorals and *latissimus dorsi*. This movement is, in fact, very similar in kinesiology to the decline press.

Parallel Bars
Starting Position

Grip the ends of a set of parallel bars with a parallel grip, your palms facing each other. Jump on the bars to a position where you are supporting your full body weight on your hands and your arms are straight along the sides of your body. If you have to, bend your knees to avoid touching your feet on the floor.

Performance

1. Bend your arms so that your elbows travel to the rear and your shoulder structure descends to the bars.
2. Descend as low as you can without losing control and then press back up to the starting point.
3. Repeat as required.

Biomechanical Tips

For proper muscle action in this movement, it is vital to keep your elbows centered above the bars at all times. For extra pectoral stress, lean forward with your upper body and flex about 10 degrees at your waist. For more triceps emphasis, do the movement with your upper body as upright as possible.

NAUTILUS FLYS

Muscles Involved: Primarily the pectorals, with secondary emphasis on the deltoids.

Nautilus
Starting Position

Slide the seat on the Nautilus chest machine up until you can sit on it. Buckle the seat belt to steady yourself in the machine. Place your forearms on the movable pads out to your sides and lightly grasp either the top or bottom set of horizontal handles attached to the pads. At the starting point, your upper arms will be parallel to the floor, your forearms at 90-degree angles to the floor, and your arms stretched as far behind your body as possible.

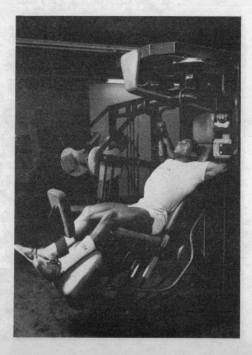

Performance

1. Push on the pads with your elbows to move them in semi-circles forward until they touch in the middle.
2. Return to the start.
3. Repeat as required.

Biomechanical Tips

You can also do this exercise one arm at a time, a practice that sometimes allows for greater mental concentration.

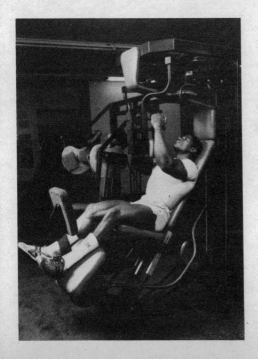

STRAIGHT-ARM
LATERAL RAISES

Muscles Involved: Primarily the pectorals when done on a flat bench, with secondary emphasis on deltoids. On an incline bench you can isolate the movement more to your upper pectorals, while on a decline bench the emphasis shifts to your lower pectorals.

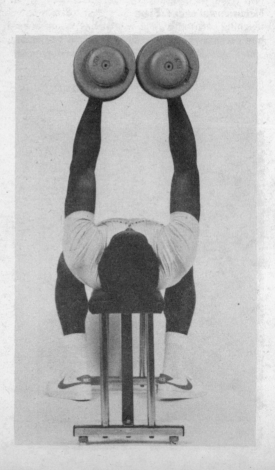

Dumbbell
Starting Position

Lie back on a flat, incline, or decline bench with your head at one end and feet flat on the floor (or knees hooked over the top of the decline bench). Grasp two dumbbells with a parallel grip. Hold them at arm's length straight over your chest, the handles parallel to each other, the inner edges of the dumbbells touching each other, and your palms facing inward. Your elbows will remain locked throughout the movement.

Performance

1. Move the dumbbells out to the sides in semicircles to as low a point as possible.
2. Return to the starting position. During the movement, your arms should be moving in a plane directly out to the sides so you are in a crucifix position at the bottom of the exercise.
3. Repeat as required.

Biomechanical Tips

Try straight-arm laterals on all three benches—flat, incline, and decline—and note how each affects your pectorals. After a few weeks of experimenting, you should be able to tell which of the three will have the most benefit in your individual sport.

Back
Exercises

POWER CLEANS

Muscles Involved: All of the back muscles, plus biceps, forearms, thighs, gluteals, and calves.

Barbell
Starting Position

Walk up to a barbell lying on the floor until your shins touch the bar. Place your feet about shoulder width apart and point your toes slightly outward. Bend down and take a shoulder-width overhand grip on the bar, palms facing your shins, elbows straight. Bend your knees until your hips are above your knees but below your shoulders. Tense your spinal muscles to arch your back slightly and look straight ahead. Keep facing forward throughout the movement.

Performance

1. In an explosive manner, start to straighten your legs to begin the barbell movement away from the floor. Be sure to keep your elbows straight at this point. They are only acting as cables to hook the barbell to your shoulders.

2. As your legs straighten, begin to extend your hips, keeping your elbows locked.

3. As your whole body reaches an erect posture, follow through on the pulling motion by rising on your toes and bending your elbows to swing the weight up to your shoulders.

4. To secure the barbell there, move your elbows under it and let the bar settle across your deltoids at the base of your neck.

5. Lower by reversing the above procedure (arms/hips/legs).

6. Repeat as required.

Biomechanical Tips

Always stick to this leg/hips/arms sequence when cleaning (pulling) a weight to your shoulders. Only by keeping your hips low and initiating the pull with your legs can you keep your lower back in the proper biomechanical position to minimize injuries. Also, with heavy weights, you will not be able to pull with arm strength if the bar has not already been accelerated by using the more powerful thighs and lower back. Remember to keep the movement explosive, or you may have difficulty getting the barbell to your shoulders. Power cleans develop explosiveness and muscle contraction speed for all athletic events.

SEATED PULLEY
ROWING

Muscles Involved: Primarily the *latissimus dorsi*, with secondary emphasis on *trapezius*, lower back, biceps, and forearms.

Free-Apparatus
Starting Position

Take a grip with your index fingers about six inches apart on the pulley handle and sit down with your feet braced on the foot bar at the edge of the bench facing the pulley. Straighten your legs to take up slack on the cable, and lean your torso forward at a 45-degree angle from the floor. Your arms should be straightened out to stretch the *latissimus* muscles.

Universal
Starting Position

The starting position on a Universal Gym is precisely like that on a free machine, except that you won't have a foot bar to brace against. To improvise a foot bar, place one or two two-by-six boards against the cross member of the machine that rests on the floor directly beneath the pulley. Brace your feet against these boards, and bend forward with your arms straight to put a stretch on your *latissimus*.

Performance

1. Simultaneously lean backward until your back is 90 degrees from the floor and bend your arms to bring the pulley handle to touch the bottom of your rib cage.
2. Return to the starting position.
3. Repeat as required.

Biomechanical Tips

The *latissimus dorsi* action pulls your upper arm bones down and back, so emphasize this motion when pulling on the handle. Also, your *latissimus* can be fully contracted only when your back is arched, so arch at the finish of each pull of the handle to your lower chest. As you pull the handle in toward your body, your elbows should be about six inches from your sides and your forearms, as nearly parallel to each other as possible. For variety you can do seated pulley rows with your palm up instead of down.

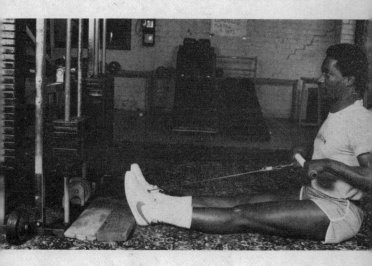

NAUTILUS ROWING MOTION

Muscles Involved: Primarily the *latissimus dorsi* and posterior deltoids, with secondary emphasis on the *trapezius*.

Nautilus Starting Position

Sit in the machine facing away from the weight stack and slide your arms between the two sets of vertical roller pads so that your elbows rest on the inner surfaces of the pads. To accomplish this may require a near crossing of your arms, but do keep them as straight as possible.

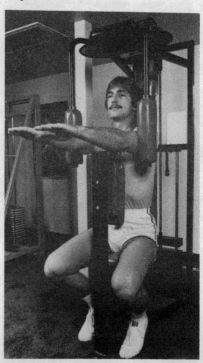

Performance

1. Move your arms straight to the rear as far as possible, being careful not to slide your elbows up or down on the pads.
2. Return to the starting position.
3. Repeat as required.

Biomechanical Tips

You should also arch your back at the completion of this movement to facilitate full contraction of the *latissimus dorsi*. Try varying your arm position occasionally by rotating your straight arms between positions with your palms down, facing each other, or facing upward.

CHINNING

Muscles Involved: Primarily the *latissimus dorsi* and biceps, with secondary emphasis on deltoids and forearms.

Chinning Bar
Starting Position

Jump up from below a high horizontal bar and grasp the bar with your hands at shoulder width, palms facing away from your body. At the start of a chin, your body will be hanging straight down from the bar, or hanging below the bar with your knees bent so that your thighs and calves form a 45-degree angle.

Performance

1. Consciously stretch your *latissimus* and then pull your body up until your chin is above the bar. Keep your legs bent as you bring your body up. Be sure to arch your back and force your elbows down and back at the top of the movement.
2. Lower to the initial position.
3. Repeat as required.

Biomechanical Tips
By varying the width of your grip, or by facing your palms toward your body, you can hit the upper back from numerous subtly different angles. By doing as many variations as possible, you will develop the best quality of pulling strength.

BENT-ARM
PULLOVERS

Muscles Involved: Primarily the *latissimus dorsi*, with secondary emphasis on pectorals, triceps, and deltoids.

Barbell
Starting Position

Lie back on a flat bench with your head extending over one end and your feet flat on the floor. Take an overhand grip, your index fingers no more than six inches apart, in the middle of a barbell that is resting across the center of your chest. Your palms will be facing forward perpendicular to the floor, your elbows pressed against your sides.

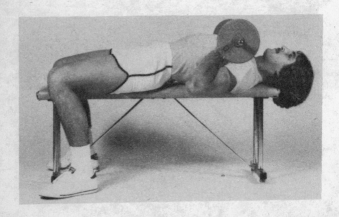

Performance

1. Move the bar back in a semicircle from your chest to a point behind and below your head that will be your full range of motion. Be sure to keep your elbows as close to each other as possible throughout the movement and the bar about an inch from your face as it passes by.
2. Pull the bar back to your chest along the same arc.
3. Repeat the movement as required.

Biomechanical Tips

Never force the barbell any lower behind your head than you are comfortably able to do. Never jerk the weight at this bottom position either, because you could conceivably dislocate your shoulder.

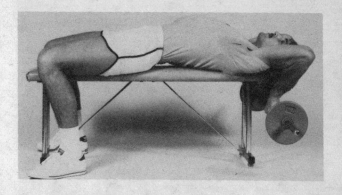

HYPEREXTENSIONS

Muscles Involved: Primarily the *erector spinae*, with secondary emphasis on the upper back, buttocks, and hamstrings.

Free-Bench
Starting Position

Get onto the hyperextension bench face down, your heels hooked securely under the smaller pads and your hips supported by the large pad. Slide forward until the top of your pelvis is directly over the front edge of the large pad. Put your hands behind your neck and interlace your fingers. Finally, sag your body forward until your torso is hanging straight down.

Performance

1. Do a reverse sit-up, arching up backward as high as possible.
2. Return to the initial position.
3. Repeat for the required number of repetitions.

Biomechanical Tips

To add resistance on this movement, simply hold a loose barbell plate behind your head as you arch up.

GOOD MORNINGS

Muscles Involved: Primarily the *erector spinae*, with secondary emphasis on the upper back, buttocks, and hamstrings.

Barbell
Starting Position

Stand erect with your feet a shoulder width apart and your toes pointed slightly outward. Place a light barbell behind your neck and across your shoulders, steadying it in that position by grasping the bar near the inner plates on each side, palms facing away from your body. Unlock your knees slightly.

Performance

1. Slowly bend forward until your torso is lower than an imaginary line drawn from your hips parallel to the floor. Be sure to keep your back muscles tensed as you descend.
2. Return to the starting point.
3. Repeat as required.

Biomechanical Tips

Unlocking your knees minimizes the possibility of lower back injury from good mornings. As you progress to heavier weights, the bar may begin to cut into your neck rather painfully. Wrapping the bar with a towel will alleviate this problem.

Shoulder
Exercises

SIDE LATERAL
RAISES

Muscles Involved: Primarily the medial deltoids, with secondary emphasis on *trapezius* and anterior deltoids.

Dumbbell
Starting Position

Stand erect with your feet shoulder width apart and your toes pointing a little outward. Grasp a dumbbell in each hand, using an overhand grip, and hang your arms directly down along your sides, elbows locked for the duration of the movement. Your palms will be facing each other.

Nautilus
Startin~ Position

Adjust the seat up until the tops of your shoulders are within an inch of the pressing handles. Sit down facing away from the weight stack, fasten the seat belt across your lap, and cross your ankles directly beneath your knees. With your palms facing each other and your hands open, slide the outside part of your lower forearm against the inside surface of the pads on each side. Grasp the handles attached to the pads to maintain this position while you are pushing against the pads with your forearms.

Performance

1. Raise your arms straight to the sides until your elbows lock and your upper arms are above an imaginary line drawn from your shoulders parallel to the floor.
2. Lower.
3. Repeat as required.

Biomechanical Tips

Little can be done to enhance the Nautilus movement, but you can vary hand positions on the dumbbell side lateral raises from palms down to palms forward to palms up. As you rotate your palms from facing down to facing up, stress is gradually moved from the medial deltoid to the anterior deltoid.

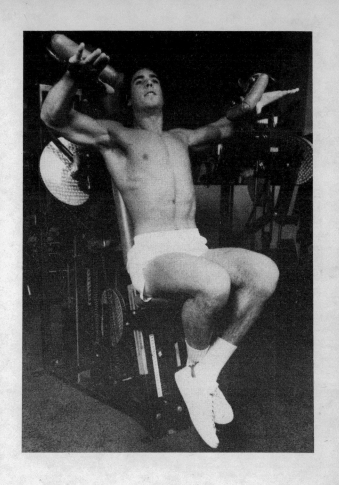

Arm
Exercises

DUMBBELL CURLS

Muscles Involved: Primarily the biceps and *brachialis*, with secondary emphasis on the forearms.

Dumbbell
Starting Position

This exercise is done precisely like the barbell curl, except that you use two dumbbells instead of a barbell. Stand erect, a dumbbell grasped with an underhand grip in each hand, your feet shoulder width apart and your toes pointed slightly outward. Your arms should be hanging straight down at your sides with your palms facing forward.

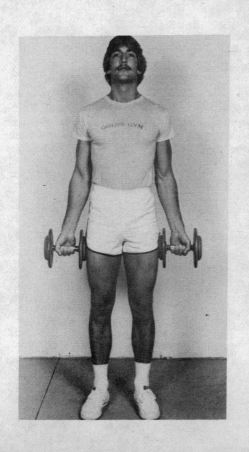

Performance

1. Pin your upper arms to your sides. With biceps power, move both dumbbells in a semicircle to your chin.
2. Lower along the same arc until the dumbbells are back at your sides.
3. Repeat as required.

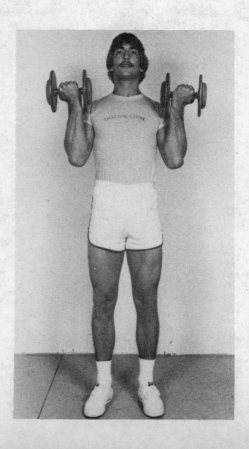

Biomechanical Tips

Try rotating your hands outward and upward at the top of the curl, which will result in a superior biceps contraction. This is called *supination*, and the biceps supinates as well as flexes the lower arm toward the upper arm. To clarify, the palm of your right hand will be facing straight forward at the beginning of a curl. As the dumbbell goes up, gradually turn your thumb out to the right until your right hand has been twisted as far as possible in a clockwise direction. At the same time, your left hand would be twisted in a counter-clockwise direction.

NAUTILUS
OVERHEAD CURLS

Muscles Involved: Primarily the biceps and *brachialis*, with secondary emphasis on the forearms.

Nautilus
Starting Position

Sit in the compound arm machine with the seat set at a level that will allow you to grasp both overhead handles while the

backs of your elbows rest comfortably inside the overhead padded cups. Buckle the seat belt and grasp the handles.

Performance

1. Curl one arm downward toward your shoulder as far as possible and then let it back up to the starting position.

2. Curl the other arm down and return.

3. Do the curls alternately, but never have both arms moving at once, because the machine is constructed to apply resistance to one arm at a time.

Biomechanical Tips

Try holding the contracted position for a moment on each repetition, and do a few partial reps (half of the way) once you are too fatigued to finish the full movement.

INCLINE
DUMBBELL CURLS

Muscles Involved: Primarily the biceps and *brachialis*, with secondary emphasis on the forearms.

Dumbbell
Starting Position

Take a dumbbell in each hand with an underhand grip and lie back on a 45-degree incline bench, your arms hanging straight down and palms facing forward. Keep your head back against the bench and your feet flat on the floor.

Performance

1. Simultaneously curl both dumbbells up to your shoulders.
2. Lower.
3. Repeat as required.

Biomechanical Tips

By lying back on an incline bench it is possible to achieve a greater stretch in the biceps, because your arms are back much farther than they are in the usual position of hanging straight down the sides of your body. In addition, this position does not allow your legs to become involved in the movement, thus restricting a larger percentage of the resistance to your biceps. As a result, you will notice that you can handle only about 90 percent of your standing dumbbell curl poundage on incline curls.

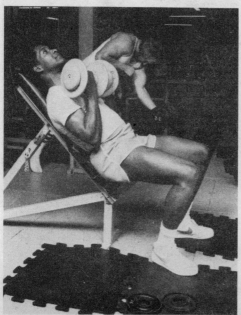

STANDING TRICEPS EXTENSIONS

Muscles Involved: Primarily the triceps, with secondary emphasis on the forearms.

Barbell
Starting Position

Take a narrow overhand grip on a barbell. Your index fingers should be no more than six inches apart, and your palms should be facing forward. Stand erect with your feet at shoulder width, toes pointed slightly outward, and swing the barbell up until your arms are extended straight overhead.

Performance

1. Lock your upper arms against the sides of your head. With your upper arms motionless, lower the bar in a semicircle by bending your elbows until the bar touches the back of your neck.
2. Return to the starting point.
3. Repeat as required.

Biomechanical Tips

Remember that your elbows shouldn't flare out and away from your head, and your upper arms must remain motionless.

INCLINE TRICEPS EXTENSIONS

Muscles Involved: Primarily the triceps, with secondary emphasis on the forearms.

Barbell
Starting Position

Lie back on a 45-degree incline bench, a barbell held with an overhand grip at straight arm's length directly over your chest. In gripping the bar, your index fingers should be no more than six inches apart and your palms should be facing forward perpendicular to the floor.

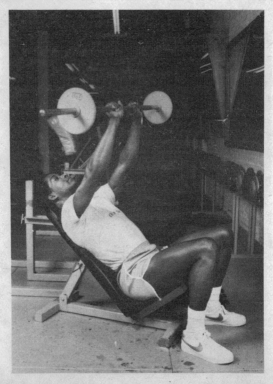

Performance

1. Keeping your upper arms totally motionless, bend your elbows and lower the barbell in a semicircle until it touches your forehead.
2. Return the barbell along the same arc to the initial position.
3. Repeat as required.

Biomechanical Tips

This movement is exactly the same as the lying or standing triceps extensions, except for the angle, so all the biomechanical tips for those two movements also apply to incline extensions.

DECLINE TRICEPS EXTENSIONS

Muscles Involved: Primarily the triceps, with secondary emphasis on the forearms.

Barbell
Starting Position

Lie back on a 30-degree decline bench with your head at the bottom end and your knees wrapped securely over the top of the bench. With an overhand grip on a barbell, hands six inches apart, extend your arms straight up over your chest, your palms facing forward.

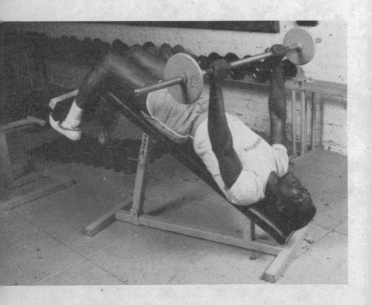

Performance

1. Keeping your upper arms stationary, bend your elbows to lower the barbell in a semicircle.
2. As soon as the barbell touches your forehead, raise it back to the starting position.
3. Repeat as required.

Biomechanical Tips

Because each of the four angles of triceps extensions—decline, flat, incline, and standing—attack your triceps from a slightly different angle, change exercises periodically to achieve more complete triceps strength development.

NAUTILUS DOWNWARD TRICEPS EXTENSIONS

Muscles Involved: Primarily the triceps, with secondary emphasis on forearms.

Nautilus Starting Position

Sit in the Nautilus arm machine with the seat adjusted to a height that allows you to fit into the triceps apparatus at your sides with the backs of your upper arms against the rear pads and forearms against the movable front pads. Extend your arms fully.

Performance

From this position, flex then extend both arms to work the triceps muscles.

Biomechanical Tips

Hold the weight in the extended position (arms straight) for one or two seconds each repetition for a greater contraction of your triceps.

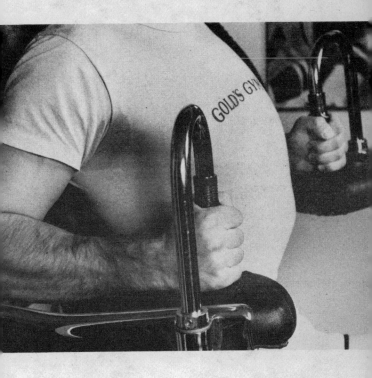

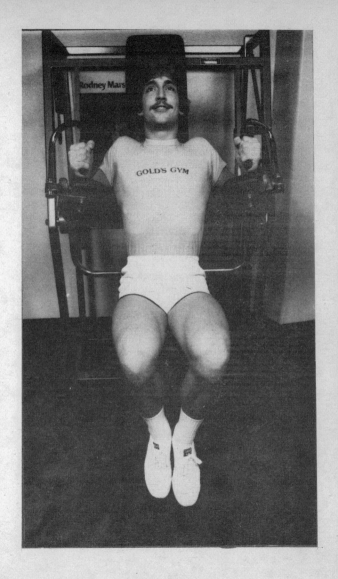

Abdominal
Exercises

TWISTING

Muscles Involved: Primarily the external obliques on the sides of your waist, with secondary emphasis on all the abdominal and lower back muscles.

Free-Barbell
Starting Position

Sit straddling a flat bench and anchor your feet in the bench legs. Place an unloaded exercise barbell or a broomstick across your shoulders in back of your neck, wrapping your arms around the bar or stick, palms facing forward.

Performance

1. Facing straight forward, steadily twist your torso as far as you can to the right.

2. Twist continuously as far as you can to the left.

3. Twist rhythmically and smoothly from side to side, counting each full cycle from right to left and back again to the right side as one repetition.

Biomechanical Tips

This exercise can also be done standing and bent over at the waist, should you desire to shift stress more to the back of the obliques, which could be advantageous in such sports as diving and gymnastics.

SIDE BENDS

Muscles Involved: Primarily the external obliques, with secondary emphasis on the rest of the abdominal and lower back muscles.

Free-Barbell
Starting Position

Stand erect with your feet a shoulder width apart and your toes pointed slightly outward. Place an unloaded exercise barbell across your shoulders behind your neck and grasp the bar out toward the ends (approximately two to two and one-half feet out to each side from the center of the bar), palms facing forward.

Performance

1. Bend as far straight to the right side as is comfortable.

2. Bend smoothly back to the left as far as you can.

3. Keep bending continuously from side to side, counting one full cycle from right to left and back to right as one repetition.

Biomechanical Tips

This is a very direct external oblique exercise, so you will never need to add weight to the bar for it. If you do, chances are that your obliques will become quite thick, thus widening your waist.

FROG KICKS

Muscles Involved: All of the frontal abdominal muscles and the gluteals, with supporting assistance from forearms.

Free-Apparatus
Starting Position

Stand below a high horizontal bar and jump up to take an overhand grip on the bar with your hands shoulder width apart and your palms facing forward. At the starting point, you will be hanging straight down below the bar with your elbows locked.

Performance

1. Keeping your legs together, pull your knees up to your chest.
2. Return to the initial position.
3. Repeat as required.

Biomechanical Tips

To attack your abdominals from slightly different angles, spread your legs different distances apart as you pull up your knees. Each leg position will hit the abdominals a little differently, and the accumulation of all possible positions will result in super abdominal strength.

Calf
Exercises

SEATED CALF
MACHINE

Muscles Involved: Primarily the *soleus* muscle of the calf, with significant emphasis on the *gastrocnemius*.

Calf Machine
Starting Position

Sit down at the seated calf machine with your toes on the foot board and knees wedged under the knee pads. Lift the weight up a couple of inches using your calf strength, and push the vertical stop bar forward to release the machine.

Performance

1. Rise up and down on your toes with the resistance provided by the machine.

2. To secure the weight at the completion of a set, simply move the stop bar back to its original position.

Biomechanical Tips

The broad *soleus* muscle under the *gastrocnemius* is fully contracted and stimulated only when you rise on your toes with a bent leg, so this is one of the few exercises in which you can do meaningful work for the *soleus*. If you don't have a seated calf machine, you can pad a barbell and rest it across your knees for a similar movement.

DONKEY CALF RAISES

Muscles Involved: All of the muscles on the backs of your lower legs.

Free-Bench
Starting Position

Bend over a flat bench from your waist until your torso is parallel to the floor and steady your torso by placing your hands—elbows locked—on the bench. Stand with your toes on a wooden block or at the edge of a raised platform on which the bench is placed. Have a partner jump up astride your hips, as if you were a horse, to provide resistance.

Performance

Rise up and down on your toes to stimulate your calves.

Biomechanical Tips

The heavier your partner, the more resistance provided, but it is necessary that he or she always sit in the same place on your back. Try to have your partner sit back as far as possible without falling off, because he or she will provide more resistance when sitting far back.

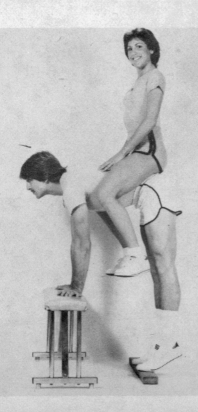

ONE-LEGGED
CALF RAISES

Muscles Involved: All of the muscles on the backs of your lower legs.

Dumbbell
Starting Position

Put one foot on a block and slide your heel out away from the block until only the ball of your foot is in contact with the block. Hold a light dumbbell in one hand on the same side as the foot in contact with the block, your arm hanging straight down at your side, your palm facing the side of your body. Balance yourself by grasping an upright post or bar with your free hand.

Performance

1. Rise up and down on the toes of one foot to stimulate your calf.
2. Switch feet for the next set.
3. Count a full group of repetitions for both legs as one full set.

Biomechanical Tips

By concentrating your attention on one leg at a time, you will often be able to obtain a better calf workout.

INTERMEDIATE STRENGTH ROUTINES

At Level Two you are ready for programs that are a little more difficult. There will be more sets per body part in each program, and of course you will be capable of using heavier weights than you did at Level One. Do each of the full programs two or three days a week, or try splitting up one according to the guidelines in the split-routine section and doing half two days a week, and the other half, two.

Free-Weight Program

Exercise	Sets	Rep Range
Squats	4	10–15
Leg Extensions	3	10–15
Leg Curls	3	10–15
Seated Pulley Rowing	3	8–12
Lat Machine Pulldowns	3	8–12
Hyperextensions	2	10–15
Incline Press	3	6–10
Parallel Bar Dips	3	8–12
Side Lateral Raises	4	10–15
Incline Dumbbell Curls	4	8–12
Incline Triceps Extensions	3	10–15
Side Bends	1	50+
Sit-Ups	1	50+
Donkey Calf Raises	5	20–30

Universal Gym Program

Exercise	Sets	Rep Range
Leg Press	4	10–15
Leg Extensions	3	10–15
Leg Curls	3	10–15
Seated Pulley Rowing	3	8–12
Lat Machine Pulldowns	3	8–12
Incline Press	3	6–10
Bench Press	3	6–10
Seated Press	2	6–10
Lat Machine Pushdowns	3	10–15
Frog Kicks	2	15–20
Calf Press	5	20–30

Nautilus Program

Exercise	Sets	Rep Range
Leg Press	2	10–15
Leg Extensions	1	10–15
Leg Curls	2	10–15
Calf Press	3	20–30
Pullovers	2	10–15
Rowing	1	10–15
Flys	1	10–15
Bench Press	2	8–12
Side Lateral Raises	1	10–15
Seated Press	1	8–12
Overhead Curls	2	10–15
Downward Triceps Extensions	2	10–15
Knee Pull-Ins	1	15–20

Barbell/Nautilus
Combined Program

Exercise	Sets	Rep Range
Calf Machine	3	20–30
One-Legged Calf Raises	2	20–30
Squats	3	10–15
Nautilus Leg Extension	1	10–15
Nautilus Leg Curls	2	10–15
Hyperextensions	1	15–20
Nautilus Pullovers	2	10–15
Seated Pulley Rowing	2	8–12
Straight-Arm Lateral Raises	3	8–12
Decline Press	2	6–10
Side Lateral Raises	3	10–15
Decline Triceps Extensions	4	8–12
Dumbbell Curls	4	8–12
Good Mornings	2	10–15
Twisting	1	50+
Sit-Ups	1	50+

Barbell/Universal Gym
Combined Program

Exercise	Sets	Rep Range
Seated Calf Machine	3	20–30
Donkey Calf Raises	3	20–30
Squats	3	10–15
Leg Extensions	2	10–15
Leg Curls	3	10–15
Seated Pulley Rowing	3	8–12
Bent-Arm Pullovers	3	8–12
Incline Press	3	6–10
Bench Press	3	6–10
Side Lateral Raises	3	10–15
Seated Press	2	6–10
Lat Machine Pushdowns	4	10–15
Twisting	1	50+
Leg Raises	1	50+

Barbell/Universal Nautilus Combined Program

Exercise	Sets	Rep Range
Calf Press	3	20–30
Seated Calf Machine	3	20–30
Nautilus Leg Press	3	15–20
Leg Extensions	2	15–20
Leg Curls	3	15–20
Power Cleans	3	6–10
Nautilus Pullovers	3	10–15
Chinning	3	8–12
Nautilus Flys	3	8–12
Incline Press	3	6–10
Nautilus Side Lateral Raises	2	10–15
Universal Seated Press	2	6–10
Lat Machine Pushdowns	4	10–15
Dumbbell Curls	4	8–12
Twisting	1	50+
Leg Raises	1	50+

Level Three: Advanced Strength Training

7

By moving into the advanced category, you will be reaching the top of the ladder in athletic strength training intensity. While bodybuilders and weight lifters will train even harder than athletes at this level, it would be useless for most athletes to train with any more intensity than we recommend at Level Three.

For the purpose of definition, we will consider the Level Three strength training athlete as one who can consistently do at least eight sets per body part (except for abdominals, which seldom need more than two to four sets per workout to reach peak strength condition). Because it takes anywhere from two or three months to a year to reach this level, don't try to rush it. Go slowly, because an excessive work volume will very quickly lead to overtraining.

Most of the exercises in this chapter will be with free weights and machines, because the number of possible exercises on Universal and Nautilus are all but exhausted. By the time you've tried the exercises in this section, you'll have a fairly large pool to choose from. This is, however, only a fraction of the number of exercises you can use. So don't be afraid to try out new ones you read about or notice other athletes doing in the weight room.

Several new training techniques will help you make the most of the advanced programs. These techniques include how to "push" in a workout, how to use preexhaustion and forced reps, and how to peak and taper with weights.

ADVANCED STRENGTH TRAINING TECHNIQUES

Pushing

Pushing is a strength training term that simply means trying hard, and it's a concept that leads to the fastest strength increases. Pushing means doing one or two more reps each time than the number at which you usually stop, and it means going for the next set before you feel you're fully rested. And it means constantly trying to add a few more pounds to each exercise.

If you don't push, you will fall far short of the strength gains possible when trying hard. The body resists having to adapt to increased work loads. And it's necessary to push hard and force the resistance up by raising the number of reps, increasing the weight used, or cutting the rest intervals.

Preexhaustion

Most basic exercises work a large muscle group in combination with a smaller muscle, for example, the *latissimus dorsi* is worked with the biceps on bent rows, and deltoids or pectorals, with the triceps on military presses or bench presses. The small muscle usually becomes fatigued before the large one when strong and weak are worked together. And when this happens, you get to a point where you complete a bench press set having fatigued your triceps before the pectorals, and often having had to stop pressing because the triceps were pushed to failure, while the deltoids or pectorals were left far from being as fatigued as the triceps. This causes the pectorals to be exercised proportionately less than the triceps.

Because the smaller and weaker muscles limit full exercise of the larger muscles, it is necessary to find a method of working the bigger groups more thoroughly than simply doing bench presses, military presses, or bent rowing. The method that has been evolved to solve this problem is called *preexhaustion*.

Preexhaustion amounts to doing a set of an isolation exercise for a large muscle group and, with no rest, doing a basic movement for the same group. Isolation exercises work a single muscle group by itself, not in combination with others. In our Level Two exercise group, side laterals are an isolation exercise for the deltoids, and flys isolate the pectorals. Basic exercises work several muscle groups in concert, for example, military presses for the deltoids and triceps, and bench presses for the pectorals, deltoids, and triceps.

What this technique does is exhaust the large muscle group with an isolation exercise to make it temporarily weaker than the smaller group, so you can push the basic movement hard enough to work the large muscle exceedingly hard. Here are examples of this preexhaustion combination of isolation exercises with basic exercises:

Latissimus dorsi—Pullovers with bent rowing or lat machine pulldowns
Deltoids—Side lateral raises with military presses or seated presses
Pectorals—Flys with bench presses
Thighs—Leg extensions with squats or leg presses

Go as quickly between the two exercises as possible, because the isolation movement does no good if the muscle is allowed to recuperate before doing the basic exercise. After this dual set, which is usually called a "superset," take a 60- to 90-second rest before doing another superset. And remember to push hard on each of the two sets.

Forced Reps

Forced reps are a method you can use to push yourself beyond your normal point of failure on an exercise. Using a training partner you can get an "assist" in finishing more repetitions than you usually do. By progressively taking off a little more weight as you tire on each rep, your partner can push you far past the point of normal fatigue so that you receive much more strength-building stimulation.

As an example of forced reps, try the bench press. Let your partner stand at the head end of the bench, as if spotting you. If you can do nine full reps by yourself, go ahead and try the tenth, and as you fail, your partner will grasp the middle of the bar and pull up just hard enough for you to finish. Do three or more such reps, with your partner pulling a little harder on each repetition.

Do between three and five forced reps at the end of a set of a basic exercise such as bench presses or lat machine pull-downs. They will give your progress a considerable boost.

Tapering and Peaking With Weights

If you peak and then taper off in your sports workouts, you should do the same in your strength training. The procedure is very similar to that used in your own sport.

During the season of your sport, we recommend only two strength training workouts per week and none the day before a competition. The length of your competitive season, of course, can vary from about three months to six or more each year. Peaking during this phase involves simply pushing harder and harder until a week to ten days before your competition. Gradually use heavier and heavier weights and perform the movements faster and faster, timing your most intense workout of the season to fall seven to ten days before your most important competition.

At the seven-to-ten day point before competing, taper off by doing two or three progressively lighter workouts at three- or four-day intervals. Do the first of these with 75 percent of your usual exercise poundages and 75 percent of the usual number of sets for each movement. For the next workout, go to a 50–50 combination, and if you do a third, go 30–30. Work a little faster each time, until you rest only 15 to 30 seconds between sets during your last strength training session.

Peaking and tapering are very advanced techniques that need to be individually determined by every athlete. Using the guidelines just presented, you can go ahead and try experiments in these areas to evolve your personal method.

LEVEL THREE
EXERCISES

This will be the last group of new exercises to add to your pool from the first and second levels. There are scores of other possible movements, so don't feel compelled to stick only to the ones in this book. As you see or hear of new exercises, you can gradually add them to your pool, too.

Chest
Exercises

NARROW-GRIP
BENCH PRESS

Muscles Involved: Primarily the pectorals and deltoids, with significant emphasis on triceps.

Barbell
Starting Position

Lie back on a flat bench with your head near one end and your feet flat on the floor. With an overhand grip in the middle of the barbell handle, hands six inches apart and palms facing

forward, extend your arms until they are locked out straight over your chest.

Performance

1. Bend your arms and lower the barbell vertically until it touches the lower part of your ribcage.
2. Push back to the starting position.
3. Repeat for the required number of sets.

Biomechanical Tips

The narrower your grip when bench pressing, the more stress is shifted to the middle part of your pectorals (the muscle nearer your sternum). With a narrower grip, the triceps also come increasingly into play.

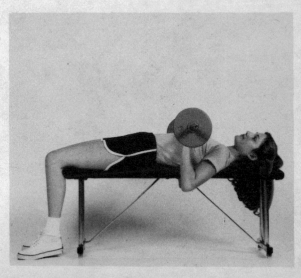

Back
Exercises

DUMBBELL BENT ROWING

Muscles Involved: Primarily the *latissimus dorsi*, with secondary emphasis on the *trapezius*, biceps, and forearms.

Dumbbell Starting Position

Stand with your feet about shoulder width apart, your toes pointed slightly outward, and your knees unlocked. Grasp two dumbbells, one in each hand, with an overhand grip, your

palms facing your shins as you are bent over with your torso parallel to the floor. Dangle the dumbbells straight down at arm's length.

Performance

1. Pull the dumbbells up to touch at the lower part of your ribcage.
2. Return them to the hanging position.
3. Repeat as required.

Biomechanical Tips

To attack the upper back from slightly different angles, try doing different sets with palms facing each other or facing toward your legs. Also pull the dumbbells to different positions on your torso, because each new position will hit the upper back a little differently.

NAUTILUS
BEHIND NECK

Muscles Involved: Primarily the *latissimus dorsi*, with a little emphasis on the triceps.

Nautilus
Starting Position

Adjust the seat so that your shoulders are directly in front of the cam pivots. Buckle in and force your elbows between the rollers with your palms facing forward.

Performance

1. Move your straight arms directly out and down to your sides in semicircles until the roller pads touch the sides of your torso.
2. Return to the starting position.
3. Repeat as required.

Biomechanical Tips

Arch your back on this exercise for a more complete *latissimus dorsi* contraction.

STRAIGHT-ARM
PULLOVERS

Muscles Involved: Primarily the *latissimus dorsi* and pectorals, with some emphasis on the *trapezius* and triceps.

Barbell
Starting Position

Lie back on a flat bench with your head near one end and your feet flat on the floor. Take an overhand grip in the middle of the barbell handle with your hands six inches apart, palms facing forward. Extend your arms until they are straight and the barbell is directly above your chest.

Performance

1. While keeping your elbows locked, allow the barbell to travel in a semicircle back and behind your head as far as it is comfortable to lower it.
2. Return along the same path to the starting position.
3. Repeat as required.

Biomechanical Tips

Each width of grip you use on this movement will result in a slightly different stress on the upper back. Try grips in width from hands touching in the middle of the bar to hands shoulder-width apart.

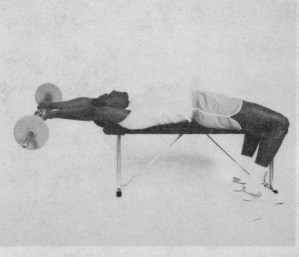

UPRIGHT ROWING

Muscles Involved: Primarily the *trapezius*, with secondary emphasis on deltoids, biceps, and forearms.

Barbell
Starting Position

Stand erect with your feet about shoulder width apart and your toes pointed slightly outward. Take a six-inch-wide overhand grip on the middle of a barbell handle, and hold the barbell across your upper thighs with straight arms. Your palms should face your body.

Universal
Starting Position

On the Universal Gym, use the low pulley station and grasp the pulley handle with your hands six inches apart and the handle resting across the tops of your thighs, palms facing your thighs.

Performance

1. Pull the bar or handle up your body to your chin, emphasizing an elbows-up position at the top of the movement. Keep the barbell or pulley handle close to your body throughout the movement, and sag your shoulders down at the beginning of each repetition.
2. Lower slowly.
3. Repeat as required.

Biomechanical Tips

It is important to tense the upper back muscles at the top of the movement by forcing your shoulders back. Keep your lower back muscles tight throughout the movement to prevent lumbar injuries.

STIFF-LEGGED DEADLIFTS

Muscles Involved: Primarily the lower back and hamstrings, with secondary emphasis on the upper back, buttocks, and forearms.

Barbell
Starting Position

Stand erect with your feet about shoulder width apart and your toes pointed slightly outward. Take an overhand grip on a barbell, palms facing your body, hands shoulder width apart. Rest the barbell across the tops of your thighs with your arms straight.

Performance

1. Keeping your knees locked, bend slowly forward at the waist as far as possible.
2. Return to the upright position.
3. Repeat as required.

Biomechanical Tips

Because lifting with legs straight puts the back in a bad bio-mechanical position, it is vital to do the reps slowly to avoid lower back strain. And because the barbell plates will touch the floor and keep the range of movement short, try standing on a flat bench or a phone book. On the bench, the plates will go below your feet, and the movement will be several inches longer.

NAUTILUS HIP
AND BACK

Muscles Involved: Primarily the lower back and buttocks, with secondary emphasis on the hamstrings.

Nautilus
Starting Position

Lie on your back in the machine with the backs of your knees draped over the rollers. Slide your hips as far toward the roller as you can, bending your knees toward your chest. Buckle the seat belt across your hips and push down on your knees to straighten them.

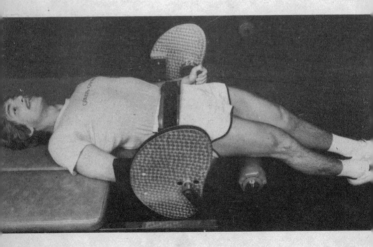

Performance

1. Bend one leg toward your chest as far as it will go and then push it back again.
2. Repeat with the other leg.
3. Alternate between the two for the required number of repetitions for each leg.

Biomechanical Tips

Arch your lower back as you do the movement, and keep your body flat on the bench. Rocking from side to side decreases the range of movement.

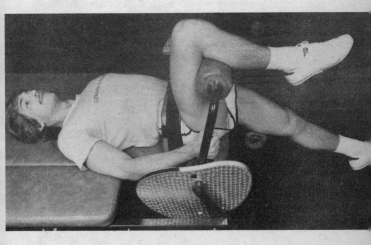

Shoulder Exercises

PRESS BEHIND NECK

Muscles Involved: Primarily the frontal deltoids, with secondary emphasis on the rest of the deltoids, triceps, and *trapezius*.

Barbell
Starting Position

Stand erect with your feet about a shoulder width apart and your toes angled slightly outward. Place a barbell behind your neck and across your shoulders, and grasp it with an overhand grip, hands about six inches wider than your shoulders on each side, palms facing forward.

Performance

1. Push the barbell straight up until your elbows lock and the weight is directly above your head.
2. Bend your elbows and return the weight to the starting point.
3. Repeat as required.

Biomechanical Tips

To make both this and the military press better exercises, remove much of the leg assistance by sitting on a bench or chair. You'll find you can use slightly less weight this way, but the benefits will be decidedly better.

BENT LATERAL
RAISES

Muscles Involved: Primarily the rear deltoids and *trapezius*, with secondary emphasis on the rest of the deltoids and *latissimus dorsi*.

Dumbbell
Starting Position

Stand with feet about shoulder width apart, and bend over at the waist until your torso is parallel to the floor. Hold a dumbbell in each hand with an overhand grip, your arms dangling straight down below your chest, and your palms facing each other. Lock your arms straight.

Performance

1. Raise the dumbbells slowly in semicircles straight out to the sides until the weights go above an imaginary line drawn from your hips parallel to the floor.
2. Lower slowly.
3. Repeat as required.

Biomechanical Tips

You can use two different hand positions, palms facing backward at the bottom and facing each other at the bottom of the exercise. Each will attack a slightly different part of the posterior deltoids.

SUPINE CURLS

Muscles Involved: Primarily the biceps and forearms.

Dumbbell
Starting Position

Lie on your back on a high flat bench, head at one end and feet flat on the floor. Grasp two dumbbells, one in each hand, with an underhand grip, and hang your arms straight down under the bench, palms forward.

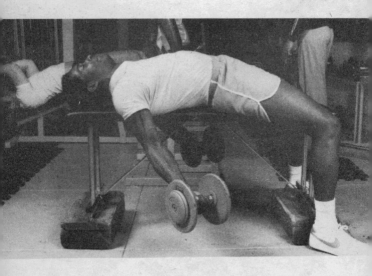

Performance

1. Curl the dumbbells up as high toward your shoulders as you can.
2. Lower to the starting point.
3. Repeat as required.

Biomechanical Tips

The advantage of curling dumbbells in this position is that a greater stretch is possible—actually necessary—at the start of the curl.

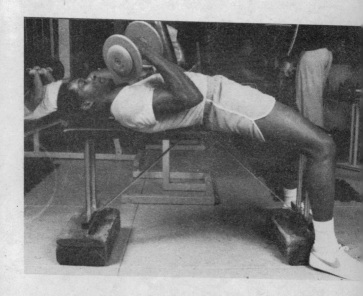

DUMBBELL KICKBACKS

Muscles Involved: Primarily the triceps, with secondary emphasis on forearms.

Dumbbell
Starting Position

Stand erect with your feet about shoulder width apart and your toes angled outward. Bend over at your waist until your torso is parallel to the floor. Grasp a dumbbell in each hand, palms facing each other, and pin your upper arms to the sides of your torso, with your upper arms parallel to the floor. Bend your elbows until your forearms are at a 45-degree angle to your upper arms.

Performance

1. Simultaneously straighten both arms out behind you until your elbows lock. Hold for a moment.
2. Return to the start.
3. Repeat as required.

Biomechanical Tips

The chief advantage of using this exercise is that—like on Nautilus machines—the maximum amount of resistance is on the triceps muscle in the contracted position, which builds superior strength.

WRIST CURLS

Muscles Involved: All of the muscles of your forearms.

Barbell
Starting Position

Sit on the end of a flat bench, your forearms resting on your thighs. Grasp a barbell in your hands with your palms up. Use a shoulder width grip and let your wrists extend beyond your knees.

Performance

1. Sag your wrists down toward the floor as far as they will go and then curl the weight up as high as you can.
2. Lower.
3. Repeat as required. Be sure you move nothing but your wrists on this exercise.

Biomechanical Tips

When you have done two or three sets of wrist curls with your palms facing up, turn your palms down and do a few more sets. You will find that you can use about half as much weight with palms down as you used with them up. Wrist curls with palms up work the insides of your forearms; those with palms down, the outsides of your forearms.

DUMBBELL
WRIST CURLS

Muscles Involved: All of the muscles of your forearms.

Dumbbell
Starting Position

Sit upright at the end of a flat bench and grasp a pair of dumbbells in your hands, palms up and forearms resting on your thighs. Your wrists should be extending past your knees.

Performance

1. Sag both wrists down toward the floor as far as possible, keeping your forearms stationary.
2. Curl both wrists up as high as possible.
3. Lower.
4. Repeat as required.

Biomechanical Tips

To concentrate better, do one arm at a time.

Abdominal Exercise

HANGING LEG RAISES

Muscles Involved: All of the frontal abdominal muscles and hip flexors (*psoas* and *iliacus*), with supporting assistance from the forearms.

Free-Apparatus Starting Position

Jump up and grasp a chinning bar with an overhand grip, your hands about a shoulder width apart and your palms facing

forward. Hang with your body straight below the bar, and point your toes.

Performance

1. Bend your legs slightly at the knees.
2. By swinging up from the waist, raise your legs until they are parallel to the floor. Throughout the movement keep your legs pressed together and slightly bent.
3. Lower to the initial position.
4. Repeat as required.

Biomechanical Tips

There is a tendency with this exercise for the body to begin swinging, which reduces the effectiveness of the movement. To keep from swinging, have a partner place his or her palm in the middle of your lower back to steady your body.

Thigh
Exercises

FRONT SQUATS

Muscles Involved: Primarily the thighs, lower back, and gluteals, with secondary emphasis on the rest of the body in a supporting capacity.

Barbell
Starting Position

Stand erect with your feet about shoulder width apart and your toes pointed slightly outward. Hold a barbell in front of your

neck and across your deltoids, steadying it by wrapping your hands around the middle of the barbell handle with an overhand grip, palms facing your body. Tighten all of your back muscles.

Performance

1. Bend your knees and sink into a deep knee bend.
2. Return to the starting position.
3. Repeat as required.

Biomechanical Tips

Keep your torso perfectly upright to avoid straining your lower back. Also, if you bend forward while squatting, you will no doubt dump the bar off your shoulders and onto the floor.

JUMPING SQUATS

Muscles Involved: Thighs, calves, lower back, and gluteals, with secondary emphasis on the rest of the body's muscles as supporting agents.

Barbell
Starting Position

Stand erect with your feet shoulder width apart and your toes pointing slightly outward. Place a barbell behind your neck and across your shoulders, steadying it in place by grasping both ends of the bar out near the inner plates with an overhand grip, palms facing forward. Tense all of your back muscles.

Performance

1. Bend your knees until your thighs pass below an imaginary line drawn from your hips parallel to the floor.
2. Return to the starting position, and as you pass through the half squat position, accelerate your rate of ascent to spring straight up off the floor.
3. Land with a slight bend in your knees to cushion the shock of landing with a heavy weight.
4. Repeat squatting and jumping as required.

Biomechanical Tips

Jump as high as you can each repetition, which will build jumping strength into your legs for high jumping or rebounding.

Neck
Exercises

NAUTILUS NECK
MACHINE

Muscles Involved: Primarily all of the muscles of the neck, with secondary emphasis on the *trapezius*.

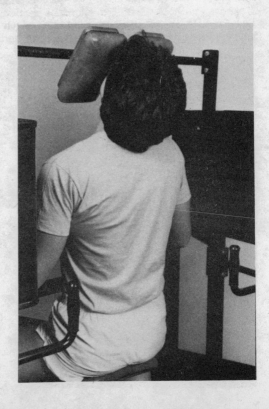

Nautilus
Starting Position

Sit facing into the machine, with the seat adjusted at a height that allows you to place the front of your head directly on the pads. Lean into the pads and let your head come forward to your chest.

Performance

1. Use your neck to move the head forward as far as possible.
2. Allow your head to return to the initial position.

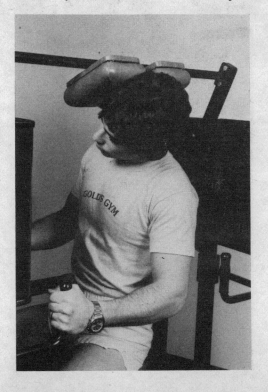

3. Repeat the movement as required. Do the same type of movement with the pads behind and on alternate sides of your head.

Biomechanical Tips

The experience at Gold's Gym has been that the neck responds best to repetitions in the 15 to 25 range.

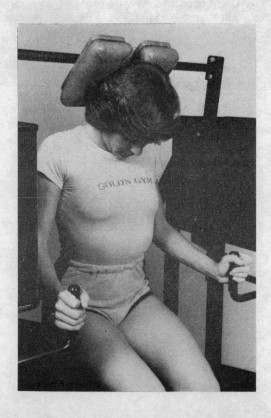

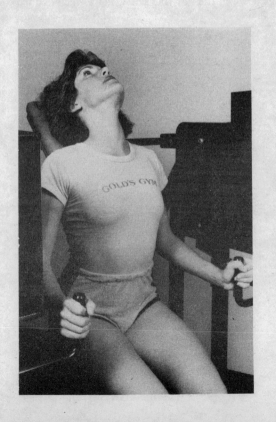

NECK STRAP

Muscles Involved: Primarily all of the muscles of the neck, with secondary emphasis on the *trapezius*.

Free Apparatus
Starting Position

Put the webbing of the neck strap on your head so that the chain hangs down in front of your chest. Put a weight on the end of the chain.

Performance

1. Move your head forward and backward as you are sitting bent over forward slightly at the waist. This will work the back of your neck.

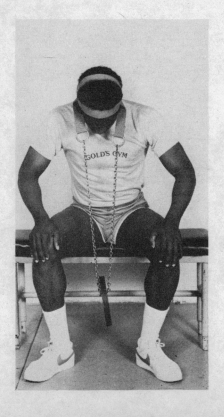

2. While sitting and bending slightly backward, run the chain down your back and work the front of your neck in the same manner as you did the back.

3. Leaning to either side, work the sides of your neck.

Biomechanical Tips

Again, use high repetitions, and work up from light weights to heavier poundages on succeeding sets.

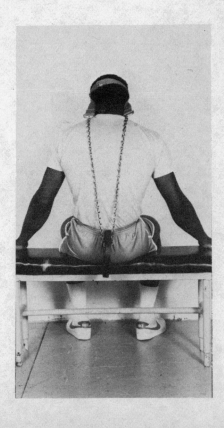

ADVANCED STRENGTH ROUTINES

This is the last level of general strength-training routines before we present the specific workouts individualized to your sport(s). These advanced routines will vastly improve your overall athletic ability; the sports routines are more specialized.

Free-Weight Program

Monday/Thursday

Exercise	Sets	Rep Range
Calf Press	4	20–30
Seated Calf Machine	4	30–50
Jumping Squats	5	10–15
Leg Extensions	3	10–15
Stiff-Legged Deadlifts	3	10–15
Dumbbell Bent Rowing	4	8–12
Straight-Arm Pullovers	4	8–12
Upright Rowing	4	8–12
Supine Curls	4	8–12
Barbell Curls	3	10–15
Hanging Leg Raises	1	15–25

Tuesday/Friday

Exercise	Sets	Rep Range
Bench Press	3	6–10
Incline Press	3	6–10
Narrow-Grip Bench Press	3	6–10
Side Lateral Raises	3	10–15
Press Behind Neck	3	6–10
Bent Lateral Raises	3	10–15
Dumbbell Kickbacks	4	10–15
Lying Triceps Extensions	3	8–12

Sit-Ups	1	50+
Dumbbell Wrist Curls	4	15–20
Neck Strap	4	15–20

Universal Gym Program

Monday/Thursday

Exercise	Sets	Rep Range
Leg Press	5	10–15
Leg Extensions	3	10–15
Leg Curls	4	10–15
Seated Pulley Rowing	5	8–12
Lat Machine Pulldowns	4	8–12
Sit-Ups	1	50+
Calf Press	5–8	20–30

Tuesday/Friday

Exercise	Sets	Rep Range
Bench Press	3	6–10
Incline Press	3	6–10
Parallel Bar Dips	3	8–12
Upright Rowing	3	8–12
Seated Press	5	6–10
Lat Machine Pushdowns	5	10–15
Leg Raises	1	50+

Nautilus Program

Note: Train on this program only three times a week, and do the series of exercises enclosed in brackets with no rest between them. The reason you need only train three times per week, as you will recall from our earlier discussion of Nautilus, lies in the superior form of exercise incorporated into the machines. Far fewer sets need be done on Nautilus than on conventional exercise models like free weights and Universal Gyms.

Exercise	Sets	Rep Range
Calf Press	4	20–30
Leg Extensions	1	10–15
Leg Press	1	10–15
Leg Curls	1	10–15
Hip and Back	1	10–15
Pullovers	1	10–15
Rowing	1	10–15
Behind Neck	1	10–15
Flys	1	10–15
Bench Press	1	6–10
Side Lateral Raises	1	10–15
Seated Press	1	6–10
Overhead Curls	1	10–15
Downward Triceps Extensions	1	10–15
Knee Pull-Ups	1	15–25
Neck Machine	4	15–20

Barbell/Universal Combined Program

Monday/Thursday

Exercise	Sets	Rep Range
Seated Calf Machine	4	20–30
Calf Press	4	20–30
Front Squats	4	10–15
Leg Press	3	10–15
Leg Curls	4	10–15
Hyperextensions	3	10–15
Upright Rowing	3	10–15
Seated Pulley Rowing	4	8–12

Exercise	Sets	Rep Range
Lat Machine Pulldowns	4	10–15
Hanging Leg Raises	2	10–20
Wrist Curls	4	15–20

Tuesday/Friday

Exercise	Sets	Rep Range
Parallel Bar Dips	3	8–12
Bench Press	3	6–10
Universal Incline Press	3	6–10
Side Lateral Raises	3	10–15
Seated Press	3	6–10
Press Behind Neck	3	10–15
Dumbbell Kickbacks	4	8–12
Decline Triceps Extensions	4	8–12
Leg Raises	2	50+
Neck Strap	4	15–20

Barbell/Nautilus Combined Program

Monday/Thursday

Exercise	Sets	Rep Range
Nautilus Flys	2	8–12
Bench Press	3	6–10
Incline Press	3	6–10
Side Lateral Raises	3	8–12
Press Behind Neck	3	6–10
Bent Lateral Raises	3	8–12
Pullovers	3	10–15
Lat Machine Pulldowns	3	8–12
Seated Pulley Rowing	3	8–12
Twisting	2	50+
Leg Raises	2	50+

Tuesday/Friday

Exercise	Sets	Rep Range
Calf Press	4	20–30
Seated Calf Machine	4	20–30
Squats	4	10–15
Leg Extensions	4	10–15
Leg Curls	5	10–15
Hyperextensions	3	15–20
Upright Rowing	3	10–15
Barbell Curls	4	8–12
Nautilus Curls	2	8–12
Lat Machine Pushdowns	4	10–15
Nautilus Triceps Extensions	2	8–12
Wrist Curls	4	15–20
Sit-Ups	2	50+

Note: On all combined programs in this book, when a choice of exercise models is available for a suggested exercise, you can choose whichever mode you like *unless* a particular mode is specified in the suggested program.

Monday/Thursday

Exercise	Sets	Rep Range
Nautilus Calf Press	2	20–30
Seated Calf Machine	3	20–30
Squats	3	10–15
Leg Press	3	10–15
Leg Extensions	3	10–15
Leg Curls	5	10–15
Hyperextensions	3	10–15
Upright Rowing	3	15–20
Pullovers	3	10–15
Nautilus Behind Neck	2	10–15
Twisting	2	50+
Sit-Ups	2	50+

Tuesday/Friday

Exercise	Sets	Rep Range
Calf Machine	4	20–30
Incline Press	4	6–10
Bench Press	3	6–10
Parallel Bar Dips	3	8–12
Side Lateral Raises	3	10–15
Press Behind Neck	4	6–10
Bent Lateral Raises	3	10–15
Lat Machine Pushdowns	4	10–15
Nautilus Triceps Extensions	4	8–12
Barbell Curls	4	8–12
Dumbbell Curls	4	8–12
Wrist Curls	4	15–20
Side Bends	2	50+

Individualized Sports Programs

We are now going to give you more than fifty strength workouts, each tailored to an individual sport, and in some instances, to specific activities within general sports categories. Certainly you will find within the following pages a program that will benefit your own athletic performance.

It should be emphasized that all programs are applicable to both male and female athletes, and all are for off-season training. Refer to Chapter 7 for the correct method of adapting off-season workouts to competitive strength training.

Each of the following training schedules is rated at the advanced level, so if you are a beginner or intermediate jumping ahead in the book, cut the sets back to your level. Beginners should be doing no more than one or two sets per exercise, and intermediates, no more than two or three sets per movement.

Serious athletes can use these suggested routines to evolve individualized training programs. Each of the routines listed in this chapter will help serious athletes make significant sports ability improvements, but only an individually formulated schedule will result.in maximum gain rates.

THE MODULE

Almost all of the workouts in this chapter are based on a "module" to which specific exercises are added. The module offers comprehensive exercise for the major muscles of the body. The additional exercises will zero in on those particular muscles with value to athletes in each listed sport. Here is the basic module we will be using:

Exercise	Sets	Rep Range
Squat or Leg Press	3	10–15
Bench Press	3	6–10
Lat Machine Pulldowns or Bent Rowing	3	8–12
Upright Rowing	3	8–12
Calf Press or Calf Machine	3	20–30
Sit-Ups or Leg Raises	1	50+

This module by itself would improve most athletes' sports performance, but with added exercises you will be able to make tremendous athletic strength gains.

To the module we will be adding several other exercises, which you can do after the module and in the order listed. And in a few instances, the program will be separate from the module. This will depend, of course, on the sport, because most will have a training routine based on the module.

THE SPORTS PROGRAMS

Aikido

Aikido requires overall body strength in moderate amounts, because most of the movements of the discipline are designed to utilize the strength of an opponent instead of the practitioner's own. Do the module exercises and the movements that follow.

Exercise	Sets	Rep Range
Military Press	2	6–10
Bent Lateral Raises	2	10–15
Side Lateral Raises	2	10–15
Lat Machine Pushdowns	3	8–12
Barbell Curls	3	8–12
Wrist Curls	4	15–20
Hyperextensions	1	15–20
Leg Extensions	3	10–15
Leg Curls	3	10–15
One-Legged Calf Raises	3	20–30

Alpine Skiing

See Skiing

Archery

Archery requires particular strength in the upper back, arms, and posterior deltoids. To develop this strength, do the module exercises and the movements listed below.

Exercise	Sets	Rep Range
Dumbbell Curls	3	8–12
Dumbbell Bent Rowing	3	8–12
Bent Lateral Raises	3	10–15
Triceps Extensions	3	8–12
Wrist Curls	4	15–20

Badminton

Badminton players need strong forearm muscles and the leg strength to stop and start suddenly. To acquire this balance of body strength, do the module exercises plus the following movements.

Exercise	Sets	Rep Range
Flys	3	8–12
Pullovers	3	10–15
Wrist Curls	4	15–20
Leg Extensions	3	10–15
Leg Curls	3	10–15
Twisting	1	50+

Baseball

Baseball requires general body strength, with emphasis on the leg muscles for running, deltoids, and forearms. To attain this strength balance in your body, do the module exercises plus the following movements.

Exercise	Sets	Rep Range
Parallel Bar Dips	3	8–12
Bent Lateral Raises	3	10–15
Triceps Extensions	3	8–12
Calf Machine	5	20–30
Twisting	3	50+
Sit-Ups	3	50+

Basketball

To become a successful basketball player, you'll need to develop your leg muscles for both running ability and jumping strength. Some added triceps and forearm strength is also necessary for optimum performance. To attain this strength balance in your body, do the module exercises and those movements listed below.

Exercise	Sets	Rep Range
Seated Calf Machine	3	20–30
Leg Extensions	3	10–15
Leg Curls	3	10–15
Triceps Extensions	3	8–12
Pullovers	3	8–12
Stiff-Legged Deadlifts	1	10–15
Wrist Curls	4	15–20

Bicycling

Strength in all of the muscles of the legs characterizes good bicycle riders, regardless of the bicycling event. Some upper body strength is also required to stabilize the body in the saddle. To attain this strength balance in your body, do the module exercises and those movements listed below.

Exercise	Sets	Rep Range
Seated Calf Machine	5	20–30
Leg Extensions	4	10–15
Leg Curls	4	10–15
Stiff-Legged Deadlifts	1	10–15
Wrist Curls	2	15–20

Bowling

Most good bowlers think strength has little to do with rolling a 300 game, but superior strength also means superior dexterity. Bowlers should have reasonably balanced strength throughout the body, with additional power in the arms and deltoids. To achieve this strength balance in your body, do the module exercises plus those movements listed below.

Exercise	Sets	Rep Range
Side Lateral Raises	2	10–15
Military Press	2	6–10
Dumbbell Curls	2	8–12
Lat Machine Pushdowns	2	8–12
Hyperextensions	2	10–15
Wrist Curls	2	15–20

Boxing

Good boxers have developed a strong punch by training against such resistance as that provided by punching a heavy bag. The punching muscles—pectorals, deltoids, and triceps—can be developed more quickly by weight training. Also vital is calf strength to keep up on the toes for each round. To develop this type of strength balance in your body, do the module exercises plus those movements listed below.

Exercise	Sets	Rep Range
Incline Press	3	6–10
Parallel Bar Dips	3	8–12
Bench Press	3	8–12
Side Lateral Raises	3	10–15
Barbell Curls	3	8–12
Lat Machine Pushdowns	2	8–12
Wrist Curls	4	15–20
Hyperextensions	1	15–20

Canoeing (Downriver)

Paddling down a river takes considerable back, shoulder, and arm strength. To achieve this strength balance in your body, do the module exercises and those movements listed below.

Exercise	Sets	Rep Range
Pullovers	3	10–15
Triceps Extensions	3	8–12
Sit-Ups	2	50+
Twisting	1	50+
Wrist Curls	2	15–20

Canoeing (Flatwater)

Competitive canoeing takes the same type of strength as downriver paddling, but in greater degrees, plus considerably more abdominal development. To achieve this strength balance in your body, do the module exercises and those movements listed below.

Exercise	Sets	Rep Range
Pullover	5	10–15
Dumbbell Bent Rowing	3	8–12
Military Press	3	6–10
Side Lateral Raises	3	10–15
Bent Lateral Raises	3	10–15
Triceps Extensions	3	8–12
Barbell Curls	3	8–12
Sit-Ups	3–5	50+
Wrist Curls	4	15–20

Climbing

Mountain climbing requires good body strength in all areas. To attain this, do the module exercises plus those movements listed below.

Exercise	Sets	Rep Range
Pulley Rowing	5	8–12
Incline Press	5	6–10
Parallel Bar Dips	3	8–12
Side Lateral Raises	2	10–15
Bent Lateral Raises	2	10–15
Barbell Curls	3	8–12
Standing Triceps Extensions	3	8–12
Leg Extensions	3	10–15
Leg Curls	3	10–15
Seated Calf Press	5	20–30
Wrist Curls	4	15–20
Sit-Ups	2	50+

Crew

Crew demands coordinated strength of the entire body, but particularly in the legs, back, and biceps. To attain this balance of strength in your body, do the module exercises and the following movements.

Exercise	Sets	Rep Range
Seated Pulley Rowing	5	10–15
Dumbbell Bent Rowing	3	10–15
Bent Lateral Raises	3	10–15
Military Press	3	8–10
Barbell Curls	5	10–15
Leg Curls	3	15–20
Leg Extensions	3	15–20
Hyperextensions	3	15–20
Upright Rowing	3	15–20
Sit-Ups	3	50+

Cross-country Skiing.

See **Nordic Skiing.**

Diving

Diving requires coordinated strength of all the body's muscles, but particularly strength in the calves, abdominals, and deltoids. To attain the balance of strength in your body for diving, do the module exercises and the following movements.

Exercise	Sets	Rep Range
Seated Calf Raises	5	20–30
Sit-Ups	3	50+
Twisting	3	50+
Leg Extensions	3	15–20
Side Lateral Raises	3	15–20

Downhill Skiing.

See Skiing.

Equestrian Events

All of the equestrian events require overall body strength, particularly in the thigh muscles. Have your coach help you decide which other body part(s) is(are) weak. Then choose one exercise for each from the group we developed in the preceding three chapters, and do three sets of 10 to 20 reps on each. For thigh strength, do three to five sets of 10 to 15 reps for the leg press.

Fencing

Leg strength and development in the pushing muscles of the upper body are important in fencing. To attain this balance of body strength, do the module exercises and those movements listed below.

Exercise	Sets	Rep Range
Parallel Bar Dips	3	8–12
Incline Press	2	8–12
Leg Extensions	2	15–20
Leg Curls	2	15–20
Squats	5	15–20
Seated Calf Machine	3	20–30
Sit-Ups	2	50+

Field Hockey

Field hockey requires strong legs and deltoids, as well as lesser amounts of strength in the upper back and abdominals. To attain this balance of strength, do the module exercises and the following movements.

Exercise	Sets	Rep Range
Seated Calf Machine	5	20–30
Leg Extensions	3	15–20
Leg Curls	3	15–20
Hyperextensions	1	15–20
Flys	2	10–15
Seated Press	2	6–10
Side Lateral Raises	2	10–15
Bent Lateral Raises	2	10–15
Barbell Curls	2	8–12
Wrist Curls	3	15–20
Sit-Ups	2	50 +

Football

Regardless of the position, football requires superior overall body strength, with particular emphasis on the legs, back, and pushing muscles. To attain this balance of strength in your body, do the module exercises and those movements that follow.

Exercise	Sets	Rep Range
Seated Calf Machine	5	20–30
Leg Extensions	3	15–20
Leg Curls	4	15–20
Stiff-Legged Deadlifts	3	10–15
Pullovers	3	10–15
Upright Rowing	4	15–20
Incline Press	5	8–12
Parallel Bar Dips	3	8–12
Seated Press	3	6–10
Triceps Extensions	3	8–12
Nautilus Neck Machine	4	15–20
Sit-Ups	2	50+

Golf

Golf has traditionally never been a sport in which strength has been important, but Gary Player, one of the PGA greats, has consistently used weight training to improve his game. Golf requires general overall strength, with emphasis on the deltoids and forearms. To attain this strength balance in your body, do the module exercises and those movements listed below.

Exercise	Sets	Rep Range
Bent Lateral Raises	3	15–20
Side Lateral Raises	3	15–20
Wrist Curls	4	20–30
Lat Machine Pushdowns	2	10–15
Dumbbell Curls	2	10–15

Gymnastics

Gymnastics events have been designed to tax all of the body's skeletal muscles, and one weak muscle group can retard progress in this sport. With your coach's assistance, determine which muscle group(s) is(are) weak, and then choose one or two exercises from each weak group from the past three chapters. Do three to five sets of each of these exercises.

Handball

Handball players need especially strong legs to stop and start quickly and change directions, as well as particular deltoid and forearm strength. To attain this balance of development, do the following exercises in addition to your module movements.

Exercise	Sets	Rep Range
Side Lateral Raises	2	15–20
Bent Lateral Raises	2	15–20
Flys	2	15–20
Lat Machine Pushdowns	2	10–15
Wrist Curls	4	20–30
Leg Extensions	2	15–20
Leg Curls	2	15–20
Seated Calf Machine	3	20–30
Hyperextensions	1	15–20
Twisting	2	50+
Sit-Ups	2	50+

Hiking

Anyone who has done extensive hiking, especially while carrying a pack frame or rucksack, will know that the legs and upper back are the first muscle groups to grow fatigued. To increase body strength in the legs and upper back, do the module exercises and the following movements.

Exercise	Sets	Rep Range
Upright Rowing	5	20–30
Incline Press	2	6–10
Leg Extensions	5	15–20
Leg Curls	3	15–20
Hyperextensions	2	15–20
Seated Calf Machine	5	20–30

Hockey

Outstanding hockey players have especially strong legs and deltoids, with secondary strength levels in arms, chest, abdominals, and back. To attain this balance of body strength, do the module exercises and those movements that follow.

Exercise	Sets	Rep Range
Flys	3	10–15
Incline Press	2	10–15
Parallel Bar Dips	2	8–12
Side Lateral Raises	3	10–15
Bent Lateral Raises	3	10–15
Lat Machine Pushdowns	3	10–15
Dumbbell Curls	3	8–12
Sit-Ups	2	50+
Twisting	2	50+
Leg Extensions	4	15–20
Leg Curls	4	15–20
Wrist Curls	4	15–20

Judo

The emphasis in judo is on strength and pulling, as well as in the legs. To attain this balance of body strength, do the module exercises and those movements that follow.

Exercise	Sets	Rep Range
Pullovers	3	10–15
Upright Rowing	3	15–20
Hyperextensions	1–2	15–20
Incline Press	3	15–20
Parallel Bar Dips	2	8–12
Barbell Curls	3	10–15
Lat Machine Pushdowns	3	10–15
Side Lateral Raises	3	10–15
Twisting	2	50 +
Leg Extensions	2	15–20
Wrist Curls	4	15–20

Karate/Kung Fu

Both karate and kung fu require good strength in the upper and lower body, with particular emphasis on the pushing muscles of the upper body (chest, shoulders, triceps). To attain this balance of body strength, do the module exercises and those movements that follow.

Exercise	Sets	Rep Range
Seated Calf Machine	3	20–30
Leg Extension	3	15–20
Incline Press	2	10–15
Parallel Bar Dips	2	8–12
Side Lateral Raises	3	10–15
Bent Lateral Raises	2	10–15
Seated Pulley Rowing	3	10–15
Barbell Curls	2	10–15
Lat Machine Pushdowns	3	10–15
Twisting	2	50+
Leg Raises	2	50+

Kayaking (Downriver)

The muscles used to paddle the kayak are the same as those needed to paddle a canoe, so do the same as for flatwater canoeing.

Kayaking (Flatwater)

The muscles used to paddle a kayak are the same as those needed to paddle a canoe, so do the same program as for flatwater canoeing.

Nordic Skiing (Cross-country)

Cross-country skiing—both touring and racing—demands strong legs and pulling muscles in the upper body. To strength train for racing, add one or two sets of each of the exercises listed below to those of the module. To improve your fitness for touring, do the module exercises, plus the following movements.

Exercise	Sets	Rep Range
Pullovers	3	10–15
Seated Pulley Rowing	3	10–15
Lat Machine Pushdowns	3	10–15
Wrist Curls	4	15–20
Leg Raises	2	50+
Leg Extensions	3	20–30
Leg Curls	3	20–30
Seated Calf Machine	3	30–50

Nordic Skiing (Jumping)

Ski jumping demands strength primarily in the legs, with a little development in the shoulders and *trapezius*. To attain the balance of strength necessary to be a good ski jumper, do the module exercises and the following movements.

Exercise	Sets	Rep Range
Hyperextensions	3	15–20
Leg Extensions	5	15–20
Leg Curls	3	15–20
Seated Calf Machine	3	20–30
Side Lateral Raises	3	15–20

Racquetball

Good racquetball players have the leg strength to stop and start suddenly while changing directions to reach the ball coming off the front wall. They also have good upper body strength, especially in the deltoids and forearms. To achieve this balance of body strength, do the module exercises and those movements that follow.

Exercise	Sets	Rep Range
Seated Calf Machine	2	20–30
Leg Extensions	2	15–20
Hyperextensions	1	10–15
Twisting	2	50+
Sit-Ups	2	50+
Flys	2	8–12
Parallel Bar Dips	1	8–12
Side Lateral Raises	2	10–15
Bent Lateral Raises	1	10–15
Lat Machine Pushdowns	2	10–15

Rugby

Rugby requires a strength balance similar to that necessary to excel at American football. This balance includes strong legs, back, and pushing muscles. To achieve this balance, do the module exercises and those movements listed below.

Exercise	Sets	Rep Range
Seated Calf Machine	5	20–30
Leg Extensions	3	15–20
Leg Curls	3	15–20
Hyperextensions	2–3	15–20
Seated Pulley Rowing	3	8–12
Upright Rowing	3	8–12
Incline Press	4	6–10
Military Press	3	6–10
Incline Triceps Extensions	3	8–12
Dumbbell Curls	3	8–12
Wrist Curls	4	15–20
Sit-Ups	3	50+

Running

Distance running demands leg muscles that can contract continually for long periods of time. Strength training helps keep the arms, shoulders, and upper back from "tying up" (tiring and cramping) during a long run or race.

Exercise	Sets	Rep Range
Upright Rowing	2	20–30
Lat Machine Pulldowns	1	20–30
Bench Press	2	20–30
Barbell Curls	1	20–30
Stiff-Legged Deadlifts	1	20–30
Sit-Ups	1	50+

Skating (Figure or Ice)

The emphasis on skating body strength is toward the legs and trunk of the body. To attain this balance, do the module exercises and those movements listed below.

Exercise	Sets	Rep Range
Leg Extensions	3	15–20
Leg Curls	3	15–20
Hyperextensions	1	15–20
Sit-Ups	2	50+
Twisting	2	50+

Skating (Roller)

Because the movements of roller skating are very similar to those of ice skating, do the ice skating programs for improved roller skating performance.

Skating (Speed)

Speed skaters have tremendously strong thighs and calves, with additional strength in the arms and shoulders. To attain this balance of strength, do the module, plus the following movements.

Exercise	Sets	Rep Range
Squats	3	15–20
Leg Extensions	5	15–20
Leg Curls	5	15–20
One-Legged Calf Raises	5–8	20–30
Hyperextensions	3	15–20
Twisting	3	50+

Skiing

Skiing—both recreationally and competitively, and in all competitive downhill events—requires particular strength in the quadriceps and trunk stabilizing muscles (abdominals and lower back). To attain this balance of strength development, do the module exercises and those movements listed below.

Exercise	Sets	Rep Range
Sit-Ups	2	50+
Hyperextensions	2	15–20
Leg Press	5	15–20
Leg Extensions	3	15–20
Leg Curls	2	15–20

Skin Diving

Swimming around under water requires pulling strength in the upper body, as well as strong legs. To attain this type of development, do the module exercises and the following movements.

Exercise	Sets	Rep Range
Seated Pulley Rowing	3	15–20
Pullovers	3	15–20
Parallel Bar Dips	3	8–12
Leg Extensions	3	10–15
Leg Curls	3	10–15
Hyperextensions	3	10–15
Seated Calf Machine	3	20–30

Soccer

Soccer is almost entirely leg oriented, although some triceps strength is helpful in developing a strong and accurate throw-in, and neck strength aids heading ability. To attain this balance of strength in your body, do the module exercises and the following movements.

Exercise	Sets	Rep Range
Pullovers	3	10–15
Triceps Extensions	2	10–15
Seated Calf Machine	5	20–30
Leg Extensions	3	10–15
Leg Curls	3	10–15
Twisting	1	50+
Neck Strap	4	15–20

Softball

Softball requires strong legs for running and upper body strength with an accent on deltoids and forearms. To attain this strength balance, do the module and the following movements.

Exercise	Sets	Rep Range
Flys	3	10–15
Parallel Bar Dips	3	8–12
Military Press	3	6–10
Side Lateral Raises	3	10–15
Bent Lateral Raises	3	10–15
Dumbbell Curls	3	8–12
Lat Machine Pushdowns	3	8–12
Twisting	2	50+
Leg Raises	2	50+
Seated Calf Machine	5	15–20
Wrist Curls	4	15–20

Squash

Squash requires strong legs to stop and start quickly while changing direction, as well as upper body strength skewed toward the deltoids. To achieve this strength balance, do the module exercises and those movements listed below.

Exercise	Sets	Rep Range
Seated Calf Machine	4	20–30
Parallel Bar Dips	2	8–12
Incline Press	2	6–10
Side Lateral Raises	4	10–15
Bent Lateral Raises	2	10–15
Hyperextensions	2	10–15
Barbell Curls	3	10–15
Lat Machine Pushdowns	3	10–15
Wrist Curls	4	20–30

Swimming

Regardless of the stroke, swimming requires whole body strength, with emphasis on the pulling muscles of the upper body. To attain that strength balance, do the module exercises and those movements listed below.

Exercise	Sets	Rep Range
Seated Pulley Rowing	3	20–30
Dumbbell Rowing	3	20–30
Pullovers	3	20–30
Parallel Bar Dips	3	10–15
Lat Machine Pushdowns	3	20–30
Hyperextensions	3	15–20
Twisting	3	50+
Sit-Ups	3	50+
Leg Extensions	3	20–30
Leg Curls	3	20–30
Seated Calf Machine	3	20–30

Tennis

Tennis requires strong legs to stop and start while changing direction, as well as upper body strength with an emphasis on deltoids and forearms. To attain this strength balance, do the module exercises and those movements listed below.

Exercise	Sets	Rep Range
Calf Machine	3	20–30
Leg Press	3	20–30
Leg Curls	1	20–30
Hyperextensions	1	10–15
Twisting	1	50+
Flys	3	10–15
Side Lateral Raises	3	10–15
Bent Lateral Raises	3	10–15
Lat Machine Pushdowns	3	10–15
Barbell Curls	3	10–15
Wrist Curls	4	15–20

Track and Field
(Decathlon/Pentathlon)

Both the decathlon and pentathlon require superior whole body development, with emphasis on the leg muscles. To attain this type of strength balance, do the module exercises and the movements listed below.

Exercise	Sets	Rep Range
Calf Press	5	20–30
Leg Press	3	20–30
Leg Extensions	3	20–30
Leg Curls	3	20–30
Hyperextensions	3	15–20
Incline Press	3	10–15
Parallel Bar Dips	2	8–12
Upright Rowing	3	15–20
Seated Pulley Rowing	3	15–20
Pullovers	2	15–20
Press Behind Neck	3	10–15
Side Lateral Raises	2	15–20
Triceps Extensions	3	10–15
Barbell Curls	3	10–15
Wrist Curls	4	15–20
Twisting	3	50+
Sit-Ups	3	50+

Track and Field
(Longer Runs)

The longer track runs demand the same muscle balance that is needed for shorter runs. To attain this balance of development, do the following exercises.

Exercise	Sets	Rep Range
Stiff-Legged Deadlifts	2	15–20
Sit-Ups	1	50+
Upright Rowing	1	20–30

338

Bench Press	1	20–30
Bent Rowing	1	20–30
Military Press	1	20–30
Barbell Curls	1	20–30

Track and Field
(Short Runs)

Sprints require tremendous leg power and supporting assistance from the upper body muscles. To attain this balance of strength development, do the module exercises and those movements listed below.

Exercise	Sets	Rep Range
Leg Press	4	15–20
Leg Curls	5	15–20
Calf Press	5	20–30
Side Lateral Raises	3	15–20
Hyperextensions	3	10–15
Sit-Ups	3	50+

Track and Field (Throws)

The throwing events in track and field require full body strength, with emphasis on the chest, deltoids, and triceps. To attain this balance of development, do the module exercises and those movements listed below.

Exercise	Sets	Rep Range
Squats	5	10–15
Leg Extensions	3	10–15
Leg Curls	3	10–15
Hyperextensions	2	10–15
Parallel Bar Dips	3	8–12
Incline Press	3	6–10
Flys	3	8–12
Pullover	3	10–15
Military Press	3	6–10
Triceps Extensions	3	8–12
Barbell Curls	3	8–12
Wrist Curls	4	15–20
Sit-Ups	3	50+
Twisting	3	50+

Volleyball

Good volleyball players have strong legs to jump vertically, and development in the throwing muscles, which are the same motivators as are used to spike a volleyball. To attain this balance of strength development, do the module exercises and those movements listed below.

Exercise	Sets	Rep Range
Leg Press	4	15–20
Calf Press	5	15–20
Hyperextensions	3	10–15
Side Lateral Raises	3	10–15
Pullovers	3	10–15
Twisting	1	50+

Water Polo

Water polo requires a combination of those strength qualities necessary for swimming and throwing. To attain this balance of strength development, do the module exercises and those movements listed below.

Exercise	Sets	Rep Range
Pullovers	3	10–15
Triceps Extensions	3	10–15
Seated Pulley Rowing	5	10–15
Leg Press	5	10–15
Leg Curls	3	10–15
Calf Press	3	20–30
Hyperextensions	3	10–15
Sit-Ups	3	50+
Twisting	3	50+

Water Skiing

Water skiing requires a combination of thigh strength and upper body power, particularly in the forearms and pulling muscles. To attain this balance of development, do the module exercises and those movements listed below.

Exercise	Sets	Rep Range
Leg Press	3	20–30
Leg Extensions	3	20–30
Leg Curls	3	20–30
Seated Pulley Rowing	3	10–15
Wrist Curls	3	15–20

Wrestling

Wrestling requires strength throughout the body, with particular emphasis on pulling power to grip opponents. To attain this balance of strength development, do the module exercises and those movements listed below.

Exercise	Sets	Rep Range
Parallel Bar Dips	5	10–15
Pullovers	3	10–15
Seated Pulley Rowing	3	10–15
Barbell Curls	3	10–15
Military Press	3	8–12
Wrist Curls	3	15–20
Squats	3	10–15
Leg Curls	3	15–20
Hyperextensions	2	15–20
Upright Rowing	3	15–20
Twisting	2	50+
Sit-Ups	3	50+

Wrist Wrestling

Wrist wrestling strength comes primarily from the upper body, particularly from the pectorals, deltoids, forearms, and biceps. To attain this balance of strength development, do the module exercises and the following movements.

Exercise	Sets	Rep Range
Bench Press	5	8–12
Military Press	3	8–12
Pullovers	4	8–12
Parallel Bar Dips	4	8–12
Barbell Curls	5	8–12
Lat Machine Pushdowns	3	8–12
Upright Rowing	5	8–12
Sit-Ups	3	50+
Wrist Curls	5	20–30

MAKING UP
YOUR OWN PROGRAM

If you don't find anything in this chapter to your liking, it's easy to formulate an individualized routine. After deciding what are the major muscle groups of importance in your sport, choose two exercises for each group from any level in Chapters 5 through 7 and do at least three and no more than five sets of each of these exercises. Then do three sets of one exercise for every remaining body part.

With few exceptions, the order in which you do the exercises is unimportant; however, when working the upper body, you should always do the upper arms after the torso. As you may remember from the preexhaustion discussion in Chapter 5, the arms are weaker than the torso and limit how hard you can work the chest, shoulders, and back. You don't want to tire them out even more by working them first. After all torso and upper arm work, do the wrist curls, because it will be difficult to grip anything after doing wrist curls.

Superstrength and Superendurance

9

Up to this point we have been concentrating on varying combinations of strength and endurance, but we will now turn to methods of developing either superstrength or superendurance with weights. In Chapter 2, it was mentioned that an individual can't develop both superior strength and superior endurance at the same time. On a strength/endurance continuum, endurance decreases as strength increases, and strength decreases as endurance increases.

So you have two options: You can combine various degrees of strength and endurance with weight training, or you can concentrate on developing one of these components to its highest degree. It is possible to point in either of these directions with strength training if either extreme strength (as for explosive events like shot putting) or extreme endurance (as for cross-country skiing) is desired.

SUPERSTRENGTH TRAINING

To gain strength you must use very heavy weights (80 to 100 percent of your maximum) for low repetitions (one to five) and a moderate number of sets (three to five) on such basic exercises as squats, bench press, deadlifts, bent rowing, barbell curls, military press, parallel bar dips, pullovers, and incline press. Your basic superstrength training routine can be varied. Pyramiding, negative movements, isometric contractions, and limited movements (all explained later in this chapter) are methods that can keep your interest level high while you increase your strength.

Basic Superstrength Training Routines

Here is a typical example of a strength training routine based on the heavy weight/low reps principle.

Monday/Thursday
Bench Press: 1 set of 5 reps at 60% of your maximum weight; 1 × 4 at 70%; 1 × 3 at 80%; 1 × 2 at 85%; 3 × 1 at 90–95%
Incline Press: 1 × 3 at 75%; 1 × 2 at 80%; 3 × 1 at 85–90%
Military Press: same as for the Incline Press
Barbell Curl: 5 × 1–3 at 80–85%

Tuesday/Friday
Squats: 1 × 5 at 50%; 1 × 5 at 60%; 1 × 4 at 70%; 1 × 3 at 80%; 5 × 2 at 90%
Bent Rowing: 5 × 1–3 at 80–85%
Upright Rowing: 5 × 5 at 75–80%
Pullovers: 5 × 5 at 75–80%
Deadlifts: 1 × 5 at 60%; 1 × 4 at 70%; 1 × 3 at 80%; 3 × 1–2 at 90%

The above system can be used with any exercises you have come to favor, as well as in any sequences or split-routine combinations you have evolved for yourself. Although the key to all superstrength training is heavy weights and low reps, if you use a maximum weight for a single repetition on any exercise more often than once every two weeks, overtraining (see Chapter 3) may be the result. If you go for singles, don't exceed 90 to 95 percent of your current limit more often than this.

Another method, *pyramiding* your reps, is an extension of

348

the typical training routine above. For that routine you increased the resistance and decreased the repetitions with each set. To pyramid, you will work the weight up and reps down in the same manner, and then continue a few sets more, reducing the weight and increasing the repetitions with each set. Pyramiding usually involves the same number of descending-weight sets as ascending-weight sets.

As an example of pyramiding, you can do bench presses with the following weights and repetitions for each set:

Bench Press: 100 × 8; 110 × 6; 120 × 4; 130 × 2; 140 × 1; 130 × 2; 120 × 4; 110 × 6; 100 × 8

The chief advantage of this type of reps/resistance is in its variety. Instead of constantly working the weight up and reps down, you can sometimes work the weights down and the reps up.

You can also experiment with *negative movements* if you can find two cooperative training partners. This technique involves having your partners raise a weight for you that's 20 to 30 percent higher than your maximum. Then, with as much control as you can muster, you lower the barbell or machine, resisting the downward movement to the limit of your strength.

To insert negatives into your routine, do them on one or two basic movements in each workout for one or two sets of three to five reps in place of one or two sets in your normal routine. Such negative movements are very valuable for strength building, but it is hard to find training partners willing to forego

their own workouts to make yours better, unless three can rotate between spotting and doing the exercises.

On the power rack (an apparatus consisting of four vertical posts with holes drilled parallel to the floor for cross pins to either hold a heavy weight at a set position or against which one can exert when doing isometrics), *isometrics* and *limited movement* work can also be of considerable value in building strength. An isometrics craze swept America in the mid-1960s and has now largely died out, but this mode of strength training does give good results and should be tried.

Isometrics involves straining against an immovable object, contracting your muscles as hard as possible for 12 to 15 seconds. This can be done by inserting an exercise bar into the holes drilled parallel to the front of your body in a power rack (see illustration). Then just contract at three positions along the movement range of one or two of your exercises. Do this in place of the equivalent free-weight exercises, but be forewarned that isometric strength is built largely in the position at which you contract.

Limited movement on a power rack is much more popular today and undoubtedly more valuable than isometrics for strength development. It involves short-range contractions

against very heavy weights of at least 50 percent more than your maximum. By setting two sets of pins in the rack (see illustration), you can move very heavy weights between the pins over a six-inch range of motion. You will be able to lift heavier weights for three different positions—start, middle, finish—of any movement than the weight you can use for the full range of movement.

After setting the pins, move the bar for two or three reps

from the bottom to the top pin, holding the last repetition against the top pin as long as possible for an isometric contraction. By doing this, you will be building a high degree of strength along the six-inch ranges of movement on which you exercise. So the value of limited movements on a power rack is greatest if you do those movements in the positions of various basic exercises where you seem to be weakest. Usually this will be at the point where the weight stops going up when you fail to finish a repetition of any exercise. Once this point has been identified, be sure one of your three contraction ranges includes it.

Anabolic Steroids

Numerous athletes—men and women—are taking anabolic steroids periodically to increase the strength and body weight. These steroids are artificial male hormones with the androgenic (associated with male secondary sex characteristics) properties controlled when the anabolic (strength-building) properties are created. Some of the most commonly used steroids include:

Orally administered
Dianabol
Anavar
Winstrol
Intramuscular Injectable
Deca-durabolin
Primobolin (from West Germany)
Trophobolin (from France)

While we do not recommend steroids, they definitely do work, despite a few studies supposedly proving they don't. Steroids help retain nitrogen in the body, and after water, nitrogen composes the largest percentage of muscle. By retaining a larger-than-usual amount of nitrogen in the body, steroids cause muscle growth and strength increases.

There are, however, numerous dangerous side effects of steroid use. As listed in the *Physicians' Desk Reference*, these include:

1. Premature bone-growth-center closure in pubertal youths
2. Testicular atrophy and decreased libido in men
3. Masculinization in women
4. Increases in blood pressure
5. Water retention
6. Possible liver and prostate cancer
7. Hair loss
8. Acne

As you can see, a couple of these contraindications are terminal.

Another common objection to anabolic steroids is on moral grounds. Anabolics are banned by every major international sports federation, because they do give athletes an edge over those who don't take them. Many argue today that if steroids were finally eliminated from sports competition, all athletes would be competing more equally than they now do with the vast majority taking anabolics. And, the argument goes, everyone would be healthier and sport, in general, purer. We endorse this view.

SUPERENDURANCE TRAINING

To build superior endurance, it's necessary to move very quickly from set to set, exercising almost constantly, using high repetitions (fifteen to thirty reps per set) with light weights that are 50 to 75 percent of your maximum. By adjusting the speed of movement between exercises, you can make the routine either aerobic (exercising within your body's abilities to supply oxygen to the exercising muscles), or anaerobic (you exceed your aerobic capacity and go into oxygen debt, using up more oxygen than your body can supply, causing you to breathe heavily to replace the used oxygen for several minutes after ceasing exercise). Both aerobic and anaerobic exercises have value in building endurance.

Aerobic exercise takes the form of steady-paced and continuous efforts, such as slow runs for long distances. When using your weights, you take rests of only five to ten seconds between sets and go continuously for at least thirty minutes at

354

a pace adjusted to your aerobic capacity.

If aerobic workouts are important for endurance, anaerobic exercise is equally vital. Endurance athletes reading this book will already recognize the necessity of periodically going anaerobic. This is usually done by training with intervals, that is, resting between sustained efforts, and it does build great endurance. With weights, simply go quickly for five to ten sets, taking no rests between sets, and then take a rest interval. Use several different exercises and rush from one to another. The weights should be heavy enough to keep you from doing more than eight to ten repetitions per exercise. Repeat this procedure of five to ten nonresting sets and then a rest interval for at least thirty minutes to achieve a training effect.

Circuit Training

The only way to build significant endurance with weights is to use circuit training, which is also the way you can do aerobic and anaerobic workouts for endurance with weights. This technique involves doing cycles of five to fifteen different exercises, going through an entire cycle before coming back to the first exercise. In such a cycle, you should choose movements related to your sport, as well as exercises for each major muscle group. Here is one typical cycle for circuit training:

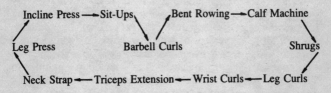

Circuit training is just a matter of starting at some point on this cycle and going through the circuit for two to five sets of each exercise to build endurance.

While it is possible to build super endurance exclusively with circuit training, we recommend that you combine it with endurance workouts in your own sport. And to peak, simply increase your speed of completion for each cycle in a progressive manner.

355

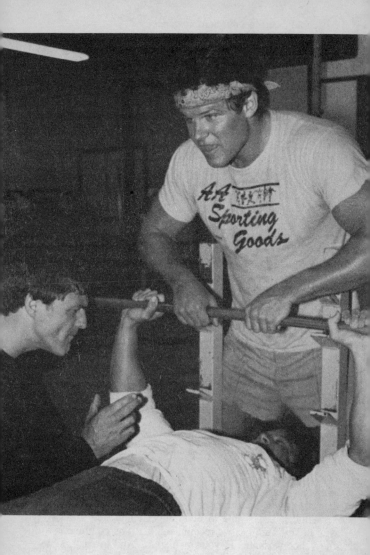

The Strength Coach

10

With strength-training techniques becoming more sophisticated each year, it is becoming increasingly difficult for most athletes to keep abreast of the new developments. Thus, they fail to receive the maximum possible benefit from strength training. The strength coach has begun to take on the responsibility of modernizing and improving weight training for many athletes.

During the 1950s, athletic coaches were convinced that strength training would ruin an athlete, but scientific studies of the relationships among strength, endurance, flexibility, and athletic ability, and the fact that good athletes of the 1950s (men such as middle-distance runner Mal Whitfield and shot-putter Otis Chandler) had weight trained, have drastically changed the picture. Now athletic coaches are eager to find out more about strength training, and experienced strength coaches have several job offers to choose from.

Typical of the new strength coaches is 25-year-old Casey Donovan, a strength coach at the University of California in Berkeley. "I am now working on my doctorate in exercise physiology," he says, "but the offers I've received for strength coaching positions are far more lucrative than what I could expect from the teaching career I'm preparing for."

At every scholastic level and at virtually all athletic clubs, there is now a strength coach, a man or woman specifically appointed to supervise the team's strength training. This coach can be a physical education teacher with this responsibility added to his or her other functions or a professional with no other duties than producing a strengthened and fit team.

At any level, strength coaches supervise athletes while they strength train. These coaches will invariably have considerable experience in training themselves and will usually be familiar with all available literature on the activity. At some levels, a bachelor's degree is required, usually in physical education with an emphasis on athletic training skills.

The more knowledgeable about strength training a coach is, the more effective he or she will be. Much of what must be known can be learned from reading books and training with weights, but knowledge of some aspects comes only with experience and numerous experiments. And even when a full body of knowledge has been accumulated, it must continually be updated, because new information is always being published.

Comments Sharon Schoenfeldt, a Washington state strength coach, "I constantly read each new article in the various athletic journals that has anything to do with strength training, physical fitness in general, or motivational techniques. And the new books on weight training all have a nugget or two of information that I can use. Some of my athletes are very well read on strength training, and I'd hate to be caught short on some new technique. I also have a responsibility to my athletes to give them the best guidance and information, which leaves them with a small edge over their opponents who might be less well trained."

As Ms. Schoenfeldt has hinted, being an effective strength coach is a challenge. He or she must be sensitive in interacting with athletes. Push some athletes too hard, and you lose their attention and trust. Go too easy on others, and the same thing happens. A strength coach must be alert to the athlete's every emotional and physical nuance. In such physical and emotional nuances lies clues to methods for tailoring workouts to individuals, as well as for motivating them. So it is essential for a strength coach to be in the weight room whenever an athlete is training.

Athletic motivation is an extremely complex subject, one on which numerous books have already been written. For a proper appreciation of the subject, we refer all readers to find *Sports Psyching* by Thomas Tutko and Umberto Tosi. While you are searching for this book, here are several practical suggestions.

Motivating athletes is a very inexact science, but nonetheless, a necessary part of preparing athletes to the maximum. At Gold's Gym we have found goal setting to be a powerful motivator.

The athlete challenged with high goals will often respond by training hard enough to reach such goals. One good goal to set is posting a lift board on which are listed the best single efforts in various categories by any team member. Many athletes will react well to this, as do others to T-shirt awards for squatting 300 or 400 pounds or benching 300. At some schools and in some clubs, making the 300-Pound Club is a highly coveted achievement.

A few athletes are self-motivators who resent a strength coach's intrusions. These athletes will progress much better on their own, so it's necessary to identify them early and adjust your approach accordingly. This type of athlete tends to be fairly introverted and to be involved in individual rather than team sports.

Donovan notes, "I've found distance runners to be the classic self-motivating athletes. They don't do too much weight work at Cal, but when they do, they're most likely to be off in a corner by themselves. Football players, on the other hand, usually like to train together and in a very open and raucous manner. They will be constantly yelling at each other during limit lifts, trying to get the most out of the athlete lifting the weight."

When it comes to motivating athletes to put forth their best efforts in the weight room, every strength coach must be an amateur psychologist. Make observations of every athlete in your charge, and talk to the other coaches to get better insights into how to handle the athlete. And above all, do everything in the weight room with a degree of humor, tact, and flexibility.

STRENGTH COACHING DUTIES

The duties of a strength coach vary from situation to situation, but all situations have much in common. All strength coaches formulate individual training routines for athletes. It's easy to make up group training programs and push groups through a workout, but a conscientious coach also works with athletes on a one-to-one basis.

Training programs are formulated only after separate analyses of each athlete's needs, taking into consideration (with the help of the athlete's coach) muscle groups that need special attention and recent injuries. The strength coach's subjective determination of the athlete's desire to succeed is also necessary before formulating an effective training routine, because a good training routine requires mental as well as physical discipline.

Whenever athletes are training in the weight room, a strength coach should be present. Even though you may be heavily insured and an athlete does legally assume certain risks when training, you and your team can be legally negligent if an athlete is injured training in an unsupervised weight room. Periodically check each athlete's form during a workout and immediately correct all biomechanical faults to prevent injuries. It will be necessary to act occasionally as a spotter if athletes are training alone. Your presence in the weight room is also valuable for athletes who will have numerous questions for you.

It is also your duty to maintain the equipment and premises under your charge. While a janitor might hurry through the weight room with a mop or broom occasionally, you'll never convince this person to pick up loose weights or replace barbells and dumbbells in their storage racks. Most athletes are equally reluctant to put away equipment in the weight room, despite the fact that they spend considerable time there, so strength coaches tend to get quite a workout just picking up stray pieces of equipment at the end of a day.

In high-use gyms, weight machines wear out and break, and barbells and dumbbells come apart. At these times, strength coaches with some mechanical ability are very valuable. Most weight machines come with repair manuals, and with experience you will begin to know what parts give out most frequently. Order replacements for them ahead of time, and you can have a machine back in action in minutes.

Schoenfeld recalls, "The first time a Universal machine broke down on me, I took the repair manual and was somewhat apprehensive about trying to fix the machine. It wasn't difficult, however, and now I know enough about it that I no longer need the manual."

The cables that move through pulleys on most machines have short life spans in high-use weight rooms. Pulley wheels and bearings usually go next, and plates in weight stacks can fracture if you allow athletes to bang the weights together when doing an exercise. Stress *control* to them.

In summary, being a strength coach can draw on every resource a man or woman can muster. While a college degree is not required, one with a concentration on anatomy, kinesiology, and exercise physiology would be helpful. In general, once you decide to become a strength coach, get all the experience you can and read everything on weight training that is available to you. Then temper this knowledge with a little humanity.

Suggested Reading

Anatomy

Gray, Henry F.R.S. *Anatomy, Descriptive and Surgical*. London: Crown Publishers, 1968.

Coaching Psychology

Tutko, Thomas A., and Tosi, Umberto. *Sports Psyching: Playing Your Best Game All of the Time*. Los Angeles, J.P. Tarcher, 1976.

Flexibility

Anderson, Bob. *Stretching*. Fullerton, Calif.: Anderson, 1975.

Injuries

Jampol, Hyman. *The Weekend Athlete's Way to a Pain-Free Monday*. Los Angeles: J.P. Tarcher, 1978.

Mirken, Gave, and Hoffman, Marshall. *Sports Medicine Book*. Boston: Little, Brown & Co., 1978.

Kinesiology

Wells, Katharine E., and Luttgens, Kathryn. *Kinesiology: Scientific Basis of Human Motion*. Philadelphia: W.B. Saunders Co., 1976.

Nutrition

Darden, Ellington. *Nutrition and Athletic Performance*. Alhambra, Calif.: Borden Publishing Co., 1976.

Morello, Joseph J., and Turchetti, Richard J. *Nutrition and the Athlete*. New York: D. Van Nostrand Reinhold Co., 1975.

Nutrition Almanac. New York: McGraw-Hill Book Co., 1975.

Physiology

Astrand, Per-Olof, and Rodahl, Kaare. *Textbook of Work Physiology*. New York: McGraw-Hill Book Co., 1977.

Strength Training

Hoffman, Bob. *Weight Training for Athletes*. New York: Ronald Press Co., 1961.

Lance, Kathryn. *Getting Strong*. New York: Bobbs-Merrill Co., 1978.

Murray, Jim, and Karpovich, Peter V. *Weight Training in Athletics*. Englewood Cliffs, New Jersey: Prentice Hall, 1956.

Randall, Bruce. *The Barbell Way to Physical Fitness*. New York: Doubleday & Co., 1970.

Reynolds, Bill. *Complete Weight Training Book*. Mountain View, Calif.: World Publications, 1976.

Riley, Daniel P., ed. *Strength Training by the Experts*. West Point, New York: Leisure Press, 1977.

Sing, Vanessa. *Lift for Life!* New York: Boulder Books, 1977.

Index

Abdominal board, use of, 118–19, 120–21
Abdominal exercises
    Level One, 118–25
    Level Two, 224–31
    Level Three, 284–85
Abdominal muscles, exercised involving, 22, 90, 92, 94, 96, 100, 126, 128, 143, 146, 148, 224, 228, 230, 284
Achilles tendon, rupture of, 68
Aikido, 307
Anabolism and exercise, 19
Archery, 308
Arm exercises
    Level One, 102–17
    Level Two, 204–23
    Level Three, 276–83
Arm muscles, 136, 148 (*see also* name of specific arm muscle)
Athletes and strength training, 2–13

Back exercises, 72
    Level One, 86–93
    Level Two, 182–99
    Level Three, 256–69
Back injury, 70–72
Back muscles, exercises involving, 24, 143, 146, 148, 182

Badminton, 308
Barbell Curls, 102–03
Barbell Curls, Reverse, 106–07
Barbell/Nautilus routines
    advanced, 301–03
    basic, 152–53
    intermediate, 241–43
Barbell Rise on Toes, 143–45
Barbells, 27–28
    bench press, 82–83
    bent-arm pullovers, 194–95
    bent rowing, 86–87
    curls, 102–03, 104–05, 106–07
    deadlifts, 92–93
    decline press, 170–73
    decline triceps extensions, 218–19
    front squats, 286–87
    good mornings, 198–99
    incline press, 166–69
    incline triceps extensions, 216–17
    jumping squats, 288–89
    lying triceps extension, 110–11
    military press, 94–95
    narrow-grip bench press, 254–55
    partial squats, 128–31
    power cleans, 182–85
    press behind neck, 270–73

reverse barbell curls, 106–07
rise on toes, 143–45
seated press, 96–99
side bends, 228–29
squats, 126–27
standing triceps extensions,
    214–15
stiff-legged deadlifts, 266–67
straight-arm pullovers, 260–61
twisting, 224–27
upright rowing, 262–65
wrist curls, 280–81
Barbell/Universal Gym routines
    advanced, 300–01
    basic, 152–53
    intermediate, 242
Bars, exercises using, 192–93,
    230–31, 284–85
Baseball, 12, 309
Basketball, 310
Beginning strength training
    program, 75–153
Belt, weight lifting, 157
Bench Press, 82–85
Bench press exercise, 63
Bench, weight training, 28, 30
    donkey calf raises, 236–37
    hyperextensions, 196–97
    knee-ups, 124–25
    straight-arm lateral raises,
        178–81
Bends, side, 228–29
Bent-Arm Pullovers, 194–95
Bent Lateral Raises, 274–75
Bent Rowing, 86–87
Biceps, exercises involving, 24, 86,
    88, 104, 106, 108, 182,
    186, 192, 204, 208, 212,
    256, 262, 276
Bicycling, 311
Board, use in exercises, 118–19,
    120–21
Bones, broken, 68
Bowling, 312
Boxing, 313
Brachialis, exercises involving, 102,
    104, 106, 108, 204, 208,
    212
Breathing, 59
Buttock muscles, exercises
    involving, 140, 196, 198,
    266, 268

Calf exercises
    Level One, 143–49
    Level Two, 232–39
Calf machine, 146, 147, 150, 152,
    153, 157, 161, 232–35
Calf muscles, exercises involving,
    24, 54, 92, 140, 143, 146,
    148, 182, 288
Calf Stretch, 54–55
Calisthenics, 9
Calories, 161, 162, 163
Calvert, Allan, 28
Canoeing, 314
Cardiorespiratory fitness, 10
Cartilage tear, 69
Catabolism and exercise, 19
Caulkins, Tracy, 11
Chandler, Otis, 357
Chest exercises
    Level One, 82–85
    Level Two, 166–81
    Level Three, 254
Chinning, 192–93
Chinning bar
    chinning exercise, 192–93
    hanging leg raises, 284–85
Cincinnati Reds, 12
Circuit training, 10, 355
Cleans, power, 182–85
Climbing, 315
Coaching, strength, 357–61
Compression, spinal, 71, 72
Contraction, muscle, 16–17
Convalescence, exercise during, 9
Crew, 316
*Crossed-Legs Hamstring Lower
    Back Stretch*, 56
Curls, 151
    barbell, 102, 103, 150, 152,
        157, 161, 162
    dumbbell, 204–07
    dumbbell wrist, 282–83
    incline dumbbell, 212–13
    leg, 140–41, 142, 150, 151,
        152, 157, 162
    Nautilus leg, 152, 153
    Nautilus overhead, 208–11
    pulley, 104, 151
    reverse barbell, 106
    seated Nautilus, 108–09
    supine, 276–77
    wrist, 280–81

366

Deadlifts, 92–93, 152
  stiff-legged, 266–67
Decathlon, 11, 338
Decline Press, 170–73
Decline Triceps Extensions, 218–19
Deltoids, exercises involving, 21,
        24, 46–47, 82–83, 94–95,
        96, 100, 166, 170, 174,
        176, 178, 190, 192, 194,
        200, 254, 262, 270, 274
Diary, training, 64–65
Diet, 10, 160–61, 162
Dips, parallel bar, 174–75
Discus throwing, 4
Dislocation of joint, 68–69
Diving, 317
Donkey Calf Raises, 236–37
Donovan, Casey, 357, 359
Dumbbell Curls, 204–07
Dumbbell Kickbacks, 278–79
Dumbbell Press, 100–01
Dumbbell Rowing, 256–57
Dumbbell Triceps Extensions,
        112–13
Dumbbell Wrist Curls, 282–83
Dumbbells, 27–28
    advantages of, 101
    bent lateral raises, 274–75
    donkey calf raises, 236–37
    curls, 204–07, 212–13,
        282–83
    kickbacks, 278–79
    press, 100–01
    rowing, 256–57
    side lateral raises, 200–03
    straight-arm lateral raises,
        178–81
    supine curls, 276–77
    triceps extensions, 112–13

Endurance and muscle strength, 24
Energy debt, 61
Equestrian events, 317
Equilibrium concept, 62–63
Erector spinae, exercises involving,
    8, 44–45, 92–93, 196, 198
Exercise, definition of, 38
Exercises (*see also* name of specific
        muscles or part of body)
    isolation, 249
    warm-up, 42–57
Extensions

decline triceps, 218–19
dumbbell triceps, 112, 113, 152
incline triceps, 216–17
leg, 136–39, 151
lying barbell triceps, 110–11
lying triceps, 150
Nautilus downward triceps, 220
Nautilus triceps, 114–15
standing triceps, 214–15
triceps, 151
External oblique muscles, 224, 228

Fat-burning strength program,
        162–63
Fatigue as cause of injuries, 6
Fencing, 318
Ferrigno, Lou, 2
Fiber, muscle, 16, 17
First aid, 69
Fixed weights, 28
Flexibility, 5–6
Flexor muscles, 21
Flys, Nautilus, 176–77
Football, 12, 320
Forearm muscles, exercises
        involving, 21, 24, 82, 86,
        88, 102, 104, 108, 110,
        112, 114, 116, 182, 186,
        192, 204, 208, 212, 214,
        216, 218, 220, 230, 256,
        262, 266, 276, 278, 280,
        282, 284
Form in strength training, 58
Foster, George, 12
Fractures, 68
Free-apparatus
    hanging leg raises, 284–85
    knee-ups, 124–25
    leg extensions, 136–39
    neck strap, 294–97
    seated pulley rowing, 186–89
Free-bench
    donkey calf raises, 236–37
    hyperextensions, 196–97
Free-Hand Squats, 50–51
Free-weight program routines
    advanced, 298–99
    basic, 150
    intermediate, 240
Free weights, 27–28, 30
    advantages and disadvantages,
        31–32

starting positions for, 77
Free-weight table, leg curls on,
    140–42
Frog Kicks, 230–31
Front Squats, 286–87

Gastrocnemius, 232
Gluteals, exercises involving, 24,
    126, 128, 132, 134, 182,
    230, 286, 288
Golf, 321
Good Mornings, 198–99
Gymnastics
    and muscle injuries, 68
    strength training for, 321

Hamstrings, exercises involving,
    92, 126, 128, 132, 140,
    196, 198, 266, 268
Hamstring stretch, 44–45, 56–57
Handball, 322
Hanging Leg Raises, 284–85
Hiking, 323
Hip extensors, exercises involving,
    92, 118, 120, 122, 284
Hip flexors, 124
Hockey, 319, 323
Home gym, 37
Horizontal bar in frog kicks,
    230–31
Hormones (*see* Steroids)
Hyperextensions, 157, 196–97
Hypertrophy of muscle, 19

Iliacus, 118, 120, 122, 124
Illness and exercise, 9
Incline Dumbbell Curls, 212–13
Incline Press, 166–69
Incline Triceps Extensions, 216–17
Injuries
    abrasion, 67
    back, 70, 72
    causes of, 6, 69
    contusion, 67
    first aid for, 69
    knee, 72–73
    muscular, 8–9
    rehabilitation after, 70, 72–73
    and safety procedures, 59–60
    sports, 6–7, 67–68
Interval, definition of, 39
Isometrics, 2, 350

Jenner, Bruce, 11
Joints
    displacement of, 68–69
    rehabilitation after injury, 70,
        72–73
Jones, Arthur, 36
Jumping Jacks, 42–43
Jumping Squats, 288–89
Judo, 324

Karate/Kung Fu, 325
Kayaking, 326
Kickbacks, dumbbell, 278–79
Kinesiology, definition of, 15
Knee injury, exercises, 72–73
Knee-Ups, 124–25

Lat machine, 30
Lat Machine Pulldowns, 88–89
Lat Machine Pushdowns, 116–17
Latissimus dorsi, exercises
    involving, 21, 24, 52, 82,
        86, 88, 90, 170, 186, 190,
        192, 194, 248, 256, 258,
        260, 274
Latissimus Dorsi *Stretch*, 52–53
Leg Curls, 140–42
Leg Extensions, 136–39
Leg muscles, 94, 100, 236
Leg Press, 132–35
Leg Raises, 118–19
Levels of strength training
    Level One, 75–153
    Level Two, 155–243
    Level Three, 247–303
Ligament tear, 69
Lower Back Hamstring Stretch,
    44–45
Lying Barbell Triceps Extension,
    110–11

Medial deltoids, 200
Metabolism, types of, 19
Military Press, 94–95
Module, basic sports program, 306
Morgan, Joe, 12
Motivation, 358–59
Movement
    definition of, 38
    limited, 350
    negative, 349–50
Muscle contraction, 16–17, 19

Muscle fiber, types of, 17
Muscle fiber ratio, 16–17, 18
Muscle groups, illustrated, 21, 22, 23
Muscle pulls, 68
Muscle strength and endurance, 24
Muscles
 bruised, 67–68
 sore, 58
 types of, 21, 24

Narrow-Grip Bench Press, 254–55
National Football League, 7
Nautilus Behind Neck, 258–59
Nautilus Downward Triceps Extensions, 220–23
Nautilus Flys, 176–77
Nautilus Hip and Back, 268–69
Nautilus Knee Pull-Ups, 122–23
Nautilus machines, 12, 31, 34–36
 advanced routines, 299–300
 advantages of, 36
 back exercise, 268–69
 bench press, 85
 calf press, 149
 chest exercise on, 84–85
 cost of, 36
 description of, 34, 36
 downward triceps extensions, 220–23
 entering or leaving, 80
 flys, 176–77
 intermediate routines, 241
 knee pull-ups, 122–23
 leg exercises, 136, 138, 139, 142
 neck exercises, 290–93
 overhead curls, 208–11
 pullovers on, 90–91
 rowing motion, 190–91
 seated curls, 108–09
 seated press using, 98, 99
 side lateral raises, 200–03
 triceps extensions, 114–15
Nautilus neck machine, 290–93
Nautilus Overhead Curls, 208–11
Nautilus Pullovers, 90–91
Nautilus Rowing Motion, 190–91
Nautilus Triceps Extensions, 114–15
Neck exercises, Level Three, 290–97

Neck muscles, 290, 294
Neck Strap, 294–97
Nordic skiing, 326

Oblique abdominals, 24
Overtraining, 9–10, 61

Parallel Bar Dips, 174–75
Partial Squats, 128–31
Peaking, 250–51
Pectorals, exercises involving, 24, 46, 82, 90, 94, 100, 166, 174, 176, 178, 194, 254, 260
Pentathlon, 338
Physical exams, 40
Pittsburgh Steelers, 12
Polo, water, 342
Posterior deltoid muscle, 88
Poundages
 increasing, 63
 starting, 76
Power Cleans, 82–85
Power rack, 350
Preexhaustion, 248–49
Press
 barbell bench, 152, 153
 behind neck, 270–73
 bench, 150, 151, 161, 162
 calf, 148–49, 151, 162
 decline, 170–73
 dumbbell, 100–01, 153
 incline, 157, 166–69
 leg, 132–33, 134–35, 151, 152, 153, 162
 military, 94–95, 150, 161
 narrow-grip bench, 254–55
 Nautilus seated, 152
 seated, 96, 99, 151, 152, 162
Programs (*see* Routines)
Progression in training, 62–63
Psoas, 118, 120, 122, 124
Pulldowns, lat machine, 88, 151, 152, 157, 162
Pulley Curls, 104–05
Pulley rowing, 186–89
Pullovers, 151
 bent-arm, 194–95
 Nautilus, 90–91, 152, 161
 straight-arm, 260–61
Pulls, muscle, 68
Pullups, knee, 151

Pushdown, lat machine, 116, 151, 153, 162
Pushing, 248
Push-Ups, 46–47
Pyramiding, 348–49

Quadriceps, 128, 132, 136

Racquetball, 328
Raises
    bent lateral, 274–75
    donkey calf, 236–37
    hanging leg, 284–85
    leg, 118–19, 150, 152
    side lateral, 200–03
    straight-arm lateral, 178–81
Rehabilitation after injury, 70
Repetition (rep)
    definition of, 20, 39
    forced, 249–50
    and guide numbers, 63
    speed, 20
    varying, 159–60
Resistance, progressive increases of, 62
Rest interval, 39, 158
Reverse curls, 106–07
Riecke, Lou, 12
Routines
    advanced strength, 298–303
    aerobic, 354–55
    anaerobic, 354–55
    basic, 150–53
    basic superstrength, 348–49
    definition of, 39
    determining, 156–58
    individualized, 345
    intermediate strength, 240–43
    split, 158–59
    to minimize weight gain, 156–58
    warm-up, 40–41
    weight gaining, 160–62
Rowing, 262–65
Rugby, 329
Running, 330

Safety precautions, 32, 59–60, 157–58 (*see also* biomechanics of each exercise)
Schedule (*see* Routines)
Schoenfeldt, Sharon, 358, 360–61

Schwarzenegger, Arnold, 1–2
Seated Calf Machine, 232–35
Seated Nautilus Curls, 108–09
Seated Press, 96–99
Seated Pulley Rowing, 186–89
Set
    definition of, 20, 39
    pump, 160
    varying, 159–60
Shorter, Frank, 17
Shoulder exercises
    Level One, 94–101
    Level Two, 200–03
    Level Three, 270–77
Side Bends, 228–29
Sit-ups, 120–21, 151, 152, 153, 157, 161, 162
Skating, 331
Skiing, 6, 326–27, 332
Skin diving, 333
Sleep, 61–62, 162
Soccer, 334
Softball, 334
Soleus, 232, 235
Specificity of strength training, 19–20
Speed and strength level, 5
Spinal compression and back problems, 72
Spitz, Mark, 11–12
Sports (*see also* name of specific sport)
    body weight economy, 156
    coaching, 358–59
    individualized programs, 305–45
    injuries, 6–7
    performance and strength training, 2–12
Spotters, 60, 157
Sprinting, 5, 17, 68
Squash, 335
Squat rack, 30–31
Squats, 126–27, 152, 157, 161
    bench, 152
    free-hand, 50–51
    front, 286–87
    jumping, 288–89
    partial, 128–31
Standing Triceps Extensions, 214–15
Steroids
    anabolic, 353

dangers of, 353–54
Stiff-Legged Deadlifts, 266–67
Straight-Arm Lateral Raises, 178–81
Straight-Arm Pullovers, 260–61
Strains, muscle, 68
Strength training (*see also* name of specific sport)
    advanced (Level Three), 247–303
    beginning (Level One), 75–153
    benefits of, 4–12
    description of, 2
    drawbacks of, 9–10
    facilities, 37–38
    and individual requirements, 64
    intermediate (Level Two), 155–243
    and speed of repetition, 20
    and sports performance, 2–12
Stretch
    crossed-legs hamstring lower back, 56–57
    latissimus dorsi, 52–53
    lower back hamstring, 44–45
    towel, 48–49
Stretches, muscle (*see* Strains)
Stretching, 41
Stretching and back problems, 72
Superset, 249
Supine Curls, 276–77
Swimming, 11–12, 336

Table, free-weight leg curl, 140–42
Tapering, weight training, 250–51
Tendon, rupture of Achilles, 68
Tennis, 337
Thigh exercises
    Level One, 126–42
    Level Three, 286–89
Thigh muscles, exercises involving, 24, 92, 126, 143, 146, 148, 182, 286, 288
Tosi, Umberto, 358
Towel Stretch, 48–49
Track and field, 338–40
Training
    circuit, 355
    diary, 64–65
    partners for, 60
    superendurance, 354–55
    superstrength, 347–52
Trapezius muscles, exercises

involving, 24, 80, 86, 93, 94, 96, 100, 186, 190, 256, 260, 262, 270, 274, 290, 294
Triceps, exercises involving, 21, 24, 46, 82, 94, 96, 100, 110, 112, 114, 116, 166, 170, 174, 194, 214, 216, 218, 220, 254, 258, 260, 270, 278
Tutko, Thomas, 358
Twisting, 224–27

Universal Gym, 12, 32–34, 52
    advanced routines, 299
    basic routines, 151
    bench press on, 83
    calf press, 148–49
    cost of, 31
    decline press, 170–73
    incline press, 166–69
    intermediate routines, 240–41
    leg press, 132–35
    leg raises, 118–19
    pulley curls, 104–05
    pushdowns, 116–17
    seated press, 96–99
    seated pulley rowing, 186–89
    sit-ups, 120–21
    upright rowing, 262–65

Vitamins, 58, 163
Volleyball, 341

Waistband, rubber, 157
Warm-up routines, 40–57
Water polo, 342
Water skiing, 343
Weight (body)
    loss, 162–63
    prevention of gain, 156–57
    and strength training, 8, 10
Weights, (*see also* Free weights)
    increasing poundages of, 63, 76–77
    tapering and peaking with, 250–51
Whitfield, Mal, 357
Work loads, progression of, 62–63
Wrestling, 344
Wrestling, wrist, 344
Wrist Curls, 380–81
Wrist extensor muscle, 106

107